Journey Th
Chakras

Dr. Ravi Ratan ☯ Dr. Minoo Ratan

Printed & Published by :
INSTITUTE OF HOLISTIC HEALTH SCIENCES
email : holihealthinst@yahoo.co.in www.aromatantra.com

JOURNEY THROUGH CHAKRAS

Dr. Ravi Ratan & Dr. Minoo Ratan
First Edition 2007
ISBN: 978 81 208 3240

Published by–
INSTITUTE OF HOLISTIC HEALTH SCIENCES, Mumbai, India
holihealthinst@yahoo.co.in / aromatantra@yahoo.com
www.aromatantra.com

Printed at–
Priya Offset, Wadala, Mumbai.

Graphics By–
Jagdeep Malhotra
Vishal printers, Mumbai–37
Email : jhmalhotra@yahoo.co.in

Cover Design By–
Yatin (Milind) Chaudhry,
yatinadvt@rediffmail.com

Marketed & Distributed By–
MOTILAL BANARSIDASS PUBLISHERS PVT. LTD.
Delhi, India. email– mlbd@vsnl.com

DEDICATION

गुरूर्ब्रम्हा, गुरूर्विष्णु, गुरूर्देवो महेश्वर : ।
गुरू साक्षात परब्रम्ह तस्मे गुरूवे नमो नमः ।।

Gurur Brahma,
Gurur Vishnu,
Guru Devo Maheshwaraiya
Guru Sakashat Per Brahma,
Tasme Shri Guruveyah Namah.

"No spiritual progress is possible without the guidance of the Guru."

This book is dedicated to all our GURUs.

कर्मण्येवाधिकारस्ते मा फलेषु कदाचन ।
मा कर्मफलहेतुर्भूर्भा ते सङ्गोऽसत्वकर्मणि ॥

Karmaneyevaadhikaaraste maa phaleshu kadaachana !
Maa karmaphalaheturbhuur ma ate sango'stvakarmani !!

Meaning:

You have a right in respect of action (work) alone, never in respect of it's fruits !
Let not the fruit of action be your motive and let there be no attachment to inaction either!!

In the Shrimad Bhagvad Gita, Lord Krishna has not only disclosed the secret of happy life but spoken about man's responsibilities and obligations, straightway to the tormented soul (ie Arjuna).

He explains the validity of the three vistas - of duty, devotion and knowledge.

It is true everybody's action is towards a desired result or goal, but the attachment to the out come of your efforts creates imbalance in the being, affecting the effort itself, resulting in imbalanced results. Therefore, you should detach yourself from the outcome of your actions, but detachment doesn't mean shirking the responsibility of your actions.

ABOUT THE AUTHORS

Dr. Ravi Ratan is a renowned aromatherapist from Mumbai, India. Author of HANDBOOK OF AROMATHERAPY and pioneer of CHAKRA HEALING & BALANCING, Dr. Ratan comes from a lineage of healers and teachers having achieved his Masters of Science (Zoology) followed by D.Sc, he runs a Mind, body Center at Mumbai along with his psycho-aromatherapist wife Dr. Minoo Ratan.

He has also done extensive clinical and research work using essential oils for health, healing and wellness, especially stress management, healing of un-healing ulcers, wounds and sores, pain management etc. In his practice of aromatherapy Dr. Ratan has combined the ancient Ayurvedic wisdom with modern aromatherapy principles and created his oil anointments for seven Chakras (the body's energy centers) which have been found very effective in restoring the healthy balance of mind, body & spirit.

Dr. Ratan also does energy field imaging before and after healing work on chakras.

Dr. Ratan is a healer and teacher par excellence. He has been conducting regular training programs and workshops in India and abroad (UK, US, Canada & UAE etc) for budding and practicing aromatherapists, healers and other health professionals in **Aromatherapy, Chakra and Crystals Healing.**

Dr. Ratan can be contacted at-
F.M's Aromatantra
C-126, Antop Hill Warehousing Complex,
VIT College Road, Wadala East,
MUMBAI-400 037, INDIA
Ph. +91-9867318010 / +91-22-24123678

email - aromatantra@yahoo.com /
        fmsaroma@yahoo.co.uk.
www.aromatantra.com

Dr. Minoo Ratan is a practicing Psycho-aromatherapist (Psychologist and Aromatherapist) and a Life coach. She is having her masters in Psychology and doctorate in treatment of Psychosomatic Disorders with aromatic essential oils. She has also been trained in advance Pranic healing with psychotherapy and EMDR (based on Shaprio School, US) for trauma management. She is a member of Bombay Psychology Association.

She provides consultancy/counseling through her center and other Institutions, for psychosomatic disorders as well as interpersonal problems (adolescent to adults). She provides treatments using Aromatherapy, Charka therapy, Pranic healing and Spiritual healings as she believes firmly in an integrated approach to health and healing.

She has been attached to SNDT University's colleges and various schools at Mumbai, India as counselor and trainer since 1997-98. She has been providing regular counseling to the students and staff members besides conducting various training workshops for them and other institutions. She conducts training Programs for AROMATHERAPY and CHAKRA THERAPY along with her aromatherapist husband Dr. Ravi Ratan.

She travels regularly to the UAE for consultations and treatments for chronic health problems.

Her clinic address is -FM's Mind Body Center, 6th Flr. Doctor House, Opp. Jaslok Hospital, 14 Pedder Road, Mumbai-26

She can be contacted for consultation appointments by mail and mobile as follows: minoo_soulstirs@yahoo.co.uk;

Table of Contents

ACKNOWLEDGEMENTS

This book couldn't have been completed without the blessings and guidance of our Gurus mainly Shri Shivkrupanand Swami and Dr. Jayant Balaji Athawale, and all the others whose guidance has helped us, in every aspect of life. We are thankful to our parents whose guidance had helped us all through our life. When we are open to learning, we get guidance from all interactions we have with friends, siblings, and especially with our students. We are thankful to all of them, mainly to our patients every where, who have so freely entrusted themselves to us.

We acknowledge the help and support of Jhon S. Rogerson who had helped us with ISIS energy field imaging system, which enabled us to authenticate our energy healing results. We also acknowledge the management and staff at Healix Wellbeing Center, Southgate, UK, specially Helena and Tal for their support and cooperation. ARE of New York (Edgar Cayce Center) had freely extended all the cooperation and support to our healing and training work, we are specially thankful to Lynn Micli, Dr. Elyce Curtis and all the volunteers at the center.

We extend our thanks to the graphic designers Yatin (Milind) Chaudhry of Yatin Advertising and Jagdeep Malhotra of Vishal Printers, for tremendous effort in graphics and lay out for this entire book. We are also thankful to Donna Fenwick, who based in New York has helped us with editing, while Vartika, Karitkeya and Devansh had helped on computation of the text.

We are grateful to the printing team of Mr. Shetty at Priya offset to complete the printing process in time.

Mr. R.P. Jain, of Motilal Banarsidas booksellers and publishers, had been a friend, philosopher and guide. He helped us with marketing and distributing our earlier book on Aromatherapy and once again he has taken up all efforts to do the same for the marketing and distribution of this book.

FOREWORD

Our spiritual quest leads us on the path of seeking the answers to certain basic questions about life, creation and God. Where do we come from and where do we go to, Minoo and myself are also seeking and simultaneously trying to share our understanding on this subject. As practitioners of holistic health we understand there is something beyond our understanding of physical self that affects the health and healthfulness of the being. Hinduism attaches as much importance to the mind and the soul, as to the body. Our health is the sum total of our life style practices and the balance of the five elements. You can enhance your health as well as longevity by drawing the optimum energy through these five elements. Ancient teachings tell us that all human actions originate in the mind. The energy is neutral and we shape it through our expression of thoughts, speech and action, empowered with strong undercurrents of our emotions.

While looking into an individual case history we try to look into various aspects of person's life style viz. physical, nutritional, mental/ emotional and social. By assessing various aspects of lifestyle we look for imbalances, as the cause of the present condition of a client. We all are aware that "Mental / Emotional" circumstances have a major influence on a person's health, besides affecting other aspects of his lifestyle. That's what we call Mind over body or psychosomatic conditions. In today's circumstances, almost all health practitioners are working on restoring health by healing the mind and emotions, but we are not always as successful, because there is still something beyond, which needs to be worked upon that is the higher mind. And the higher mind has to be worked at subtle level that's where our spiritual life style comes into focus. All spiritual books and guides suggest that we are energy bodies and connected to the consciousness or universal energy, the source or the God.

The subtle body is composed of seven major charkas or vortices of spinning energy in continuous interplay with the universal energy. Chakras are described as energy centers of our body, influencing functions of various glands and organs. These charkas are transfer points for our thoughts, emotions and physical functioning of specific endocrine glands. When we are balanced and acquire self discipline, our charkas pulsate with light, but when our emotions are blocked they become dull and sluggish. These are in practice, the ones responsible for the spiritual evolution of the 'being' through harmonious health in body, mind and spirit. CHAKRAS open and close according to our emotions and our state of mind but regulated by a higher mind.

From the spiritual point of view, Chakras are best understood as levels of consciousness, impurities have to be understood from the level of discrimination not morality. Impurities arise out of desire, self gratification and self interest. There is much more to life than fame, fortune, status, authority and attachments to things or people. All pain comes to us through ignorance and staying blind when experience tells us something different. Spiritual practices lead us to a path of righteousness and going beyond self.

In our healing practice we had been working on Chakras, using essential oils, crystals, pranic and other energy healings techniques besides mantras and spiritual therapy. This book is an attempt to share our understanding of Chakras and interpretation of life and healthfulness from a different perspective involving spiritual and metaphysical aspects of life. Since, path of spirituality is rather subjective in nature and each individual's experience may and may not be the same, therefore we do not expect all the readers to subscribe or endorse to our views.

Ravi Ratan

Introduction

"CHAKRA" in Sanskrit means a wheel that spins, in Tantric context the term is used to describe the energy centers in our body. Though in ancient texts like Vedas and Upanishads there is only a little written reference to the term Kundalini and Chakras, as most of the knowledge, had been passed on, through Guru- shisya (disciple) lineage. In recent times the interest in Tantra had increased substantially, more so in Kundalini and Chakras. So we have proliferation of literature and Institutions providing knowledge and guidelines on Kundalini awakening and Chakra opening processes. Through this book we have tried to offer a balanced perspective of Chakras from ancient Indian spiritual and tantric, as well as metaphysical aspects of the subject.

First of all, there are people who question the very existence of Kundalini and Chakras, while some give more importance to Kundailini and may agree with the existence of Chakras, but of little importance. However, from a healer's perspective they are more important for maintaining optimum health at any give time. Healers and alternative practitioners all over the world are using various ways to heal and balance the Chakras, in different practices they talk of different numbers and location of the Chakras. They may all be correct, from their understanding since it is all experiential and very subjective.

We are all energy bodies and Chakras are considered to be the transfer points of energy. To sustain the physical body we require energy, which is received through five elements – earth (food), water, fire, air and ether, energy when consumed in one form released in another form specially from major organs in bigger clusters, viewed as Chakras. Therefore, ancient Indian texts describe seven major Chakras located in the region of the head and the torso, representing activities of our major organs and glands.

Evolution is a universal process, all life is evolving and man is no exception. The human being is evolving not only as an individual only but also as a race. Mooladhar is our basic and most fundamental charka, from where our evolution begins and culminates at Sahasrara, the Crown chakra. Mooladhar or base root Chakra is located at the pelvic floor and corresponds to coccygeal plexus. In males it is located between anus and genitals while in females it is located at the posterior surface of the cervix. As the name suggests this chakra is the foundation of the physical body in realm of existence. During the process of spiritual evolution in man he goes beyond animal consciousness on to be a real human. There are certain minor Chakras from Mooladhar down to the heels, responsible for the development of animal and human instincts and intellect. This Chakra is responsible for survival and maintenance of the physical body as source of physical energy and regulates all excretory functions.

Located at the lowest point of spinal column, corresponding to our sacral plexus of nerves in the pubic region is Swadhisthan or Sacral Chakra, represents our desire center and seat of emotions. This Chakra is responsible for procreation and exchange of sexual energy and controls the unconscious in human beings. Manipura Chakra, in the naval region corresponds to Solar plexus; it controls the entire process of digestion, assimilation and temperature regulation in the body. This Chakra is also considered as the seat of EGO in human beings, as this Chakra is also responsible for the mental power and authority in all forms.

The first three Chakras take care of the basic needs of all human beings, as described by renowned psychologist Abraham Maslow, in his hierarchy of needs. Only after fulfillment of basic needs man thinks of self actualization. Same way, in spiritual and tantric practices it is said that till the time we are stuck in mundane or struggling with the basic needs only, Kundalini keeps going up to third (Manipura) Chakra and returns to the Mooladhar Chakra, only when it crosses the astral bridge between Manipura and Anahat (Heart) Chakra its movement is only upwards.

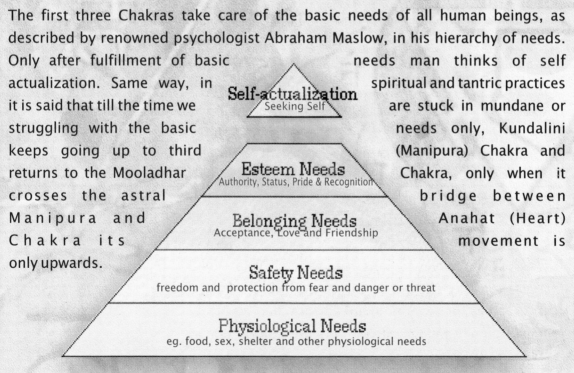

Hierarcy of Human Needs by Abraham Maslow

At the center of the chest, at the level of depression in the sternum is located our Heart or Anahata Chakra, it corresponds to the cardiac plexus of nerves and regulates the functions of the heart, the lungs, the diaphragm and other organs in this region of the body. This Chakra denotes the expression of love and empathy for all. Vishuddha Chakra is located in the deep of the throat corresponds to the cervical plexus of nerves. Responsible for communication and self expression, it regulates entire thyroid complex, certain systems of articulation, upper palate and epiglottis.

Tantra and yoga believe that Ajna or Third eye Chakra located between the brows in the forehead, is the command center. Also referred as Guru (the guiding principle), it has complete control over all the functions of the disciple's life. The aforesaid six Chakras serve as triggers of energy to different part of brain channeled through various nadis (channels or conduits of energy/prana).

As per Kundalini yoga there are two higher illuminated centers called bindu and Sahasrara. Bindu is located at the top back of the head where Hindu Brahmins keep a tuft of hair, it feeds the optic nerve and considered as the seat of nectar- "Ama-kala" the true philosophers stone of immortality.

From Ajna one moves to Sahasrara which is located a little above the fontelle. Sahasrara is supreme, considered as the seventh major Chakra, it is the final culmination of Kundalini Shakti. It is the seat of higher awareness.

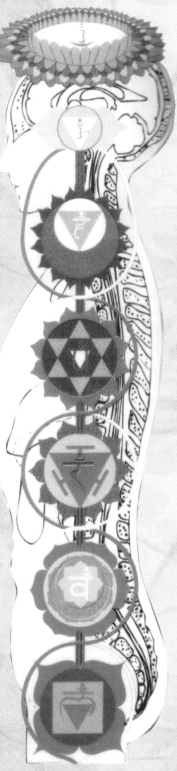

SAHASRARA

MULADHARA

AJNA

SWADHISTHAN

VISHUDDHI

MANIPURA

ANAHATA

During the process of evolution we have outer experiences, sometimes coming in our way, and inner experiences (anubhuti) through our spiritual practices, yoga and meditations, enabling different capacities and centers awaken progressively. During this process of evolution, when the Chakras get activated, our values in life, our perception also change, resulting in the improvement of the quality of love, relationships and compassion. In true sense the world remains the same but our perception of the world changes, resulting in a state of eternal peace and bliss within ie **SAT–CHIT–ANAND.**

NATURE & CONCIOUSNESS

The universe is the interplay of two fundamental principles– Nature and the Supreme consciousness, two sides of the same coin. The supreme consciousness (Purush– the masculine principle) pervading all the things, is the sustainer and the only one sign of divinity. This consciousness is the ultimate out of which and by whose power, mind and matter proceed. While Nature (Prakruti) is the feminine principle, material form of the same consciousness, responsible for procreation referred to as "Shakti" in Indian tantric and spiritual texts, as Shiva's consort. Consciousness exists in all forms of life, does not differentiate between people or species. It is the very basis of creation, the power of evolution. The consciousness of a living being is conditioned by the matter, which makes up our body. As long as we have a physical body, we participate in the play of nature, that's Maya. No incarnate body can be completely worldly or completely spiritual, no matter whatever level of light or spirituality you attain you are not able to transcend your dark side as long as you are embodied. The expression of Shakti in physical body is prana, the vital life force, which keeps this body, mind and spirit working as a complete whole or a unit.

Cosmos is the body of the Absolute, the vessel through which the Absolute expresses itself. Every created thing in the universe contains at least a spark of the universal consciousness but everything cannot express this consciousness present in them.Life, creation, evolution are the stages in the unfoldment of consciousness. Evolution is a manifestation of latent potentials through consciousness.
The ancient law of Microcosm and Macrocosm tells us there is no real difference between the vast external universe and the limited internal universe of the human body, except that the individual believes itself to be different. A human being is a living microcosm of the universe and universe is a living macrocosm of a human being. Each cosmos affects the other. Universe affects us moment to moment, and each one of us by our actions influence the entire cosmos, for good or bad. Man as microcosm contains within itself all elements, mineral, vegetable and animal kingdom. In the same way within the plant is the potential of human being.Life is rational, interdependent, inter connected, a system of mutual nourishment and care. Independence and individuality are myths of human origin.

In essence, cosmic consciousness and individual consciousness are one. While the power of cosmic consciousness or CHITSHAKTI identifies with the unmanifested absolute and the power of individual consciousness or MAYASHAKTI identifies with the world, the manifestation of the absolute. Individual consciousness is a partial expression of cosmic consciousness. These two aspects of consciousness cannot exist without one another, in the grossest of the matter there is a spark of the absolute. Same way, in the highest state of consciousness there is a particle of Maya or unconsciousness, at least a sense of individuality, because physical or gross form identifies with the material world only. Once you understand the truth of the universe, you forget your own individuality and remember your true nature. The one exists in all, and all defines the One, unity and duality both exist simultaneously. Wherever Chitshakti is displayed, there is intelligence and sensation otherwise there is ignorance and insensitivity.

Human body is like a vessel, in which there is continuous inflow of consciousness, according to individual capacity, filling the body via nervous system. The chief centers of consciousness in human beings are found in the cerebrospinal system and in the upper brain. The cerebrospinal system is the first part of the body to be developed after conception, from it entire bodily form materializes. The spine and spinal cord extend consciousness from the brain, the seat of highest awareness, (which represents our Third Eye or Ajna Chakra), to the coccyx, the pole of greatest density (represented in our Mooladhar or base root charka). At the base of the subtle spinal cord, described as Shushumna in the subtle body, lies the dormant energy unavailable to the individual, as long as his or her consciousness remains firmly entrenched in the mundane. This energy is our personal fragment of the cosmic power of self identification represented in our EGO or I-ness or Ahemkara. While the discrimination is the main characteristic of the intellect, possessiveness is the chief characteristic of Ego, which reminds you of your self-definition, and self identifies with every cell of your body from conception until death.

The more you identify with your individuality more you reflect your microcosm or the MAYA Shakti. As you identify less with your individuality, you reflect more of the macrocosm reflecting your Chit Shakti. Maya Shakti keeps you awake to the world asleep to the absolute, while the Chit Shakti keeps you awake to the absolute reality and puts you to sleep to worldly matters.

UNIVERSAL/ HUMAN ENERGY (Prana, Chi or Ki)

Our universe is primarily manifested through the interplay of unmanifested energy thus creating a vibrational field, wherein all forms are manifested energy mass, resulting out of a definite interplay of vibrations and their frequencies. Scientifically, everything living or non living, can be viewed as atom, formed of a nucleus having proton (with positive charge) and neutrons, around this nucleus is orbiting an electron (with negative Charge). What differentiates between things in the universe is the level of energy.

Human energy field is the manifestation of universal energy, it can be described as luminous body that surrounds and interpenetrates the physical body. Ancient Indian seers speak of a universal energy called prana, this vital energy is seen as the basic constituent and source of all life. The Chinese called this vital energy as Chi. Kabbalah, the Jewish mystical theosophy refer these to astral lights. All other spiritual and religious traditions have mentioned about the auric layers and depicted as light around people. Christian religious paintings portray Jesus and other spiritual figures surrounded by fields of light. In fact aura is that part of universal energy associated with objects and the same universal energy associated with the human body is called human aura.

Thus we have the "Universal Energy Field" (UEF) and "Human Energy field" (HEF). The UEF has been recognized and accepted through the ages in all cultures. The human energy field (HEF) commonly called as Aura or the biopalsmic body, has in recent time caught much of our attention and intrigued the healers and healed both. The idea of HEF being a manifestation of the UEF is closely involved and ultimately stands responsible for the harmonious balance to be created, maintained and eventually sustained to result in good health.

The idea of a universal energy pervading all nature has been held by many western scientific minds and records of this perceived energy were found in Pythagorean literature around 500 BC. Twelfth Century scholars, Boirac and Liebeault reported that the humans have an energy that can cause an interaction even from a distance. Accordingly, one person can have a healthful or unhealthful effect on another simply by his presence. In 1737, Kirlian couple, in Russia developed a photographic system to photograph human body, enveloped in the luminous aura, they could even photograph similar luminous energy field around fruits, vegetables and even non living things. In 1911, Dr. William Kilner a medical doctor reported seeing human energy through coloured screen and

filters. He described seeing aura as glowing mist around the whole body which can be described as three zones: a quarter inch dark layer closest to skin surrounded by an inch wide vapourous layer, streaming perpendicularly from the body, followed towards the exterior, by a still delicate luminosity of around six inches across. According to him, aura differs from subject to subject depending on age, sex, mental ability and health. He could diagnose diseases seeing the variation and patches in their aura.

Over a period of time many scientists, doctors, psychiatrists and healers have h, in studied and experimented with human energy field using electronic, medical instruments and even clairvoyance to observe energy patterns and making. diagnosis of physical, physiological and mental ailments, thereby giving clear indications that the electromagnetic and light emissions from human body are closely related to their health. One of the most significant works in this field had been by Dr. Valorie Hunt, who had been conducting research work showing colour and frequency correlations. In a series of experiments recording frequency and wave patterns from different body parts, Dr. Hunt and associates concluded that auric colours correlated with the same frequency wave pattern. Their research, in Feb. 1988, showed following colour / frequency correlations, (measured in Hertz or cycles per second – Hz.) these explained that these frequency bands, except for extra bands at blue and violet, are in reverse order of rainbow colour sequence:–

BLUE	250– 275 Hz. Plus 1200
GREEN	250–475 Hz.
YELLOW	500–700 Hz.
Orange	950–1050 Hz.
RED	1000– 1200 Hz.
VIOLET	1000– 2000 plus 300–400, 600–800 Hz.
WHITE	1100–2000 Hz.

Dr. Valorie stated, that frequently colours, metaphysical Muladhar/ red, Sacral– Spleen/ solar yellow, Heart– Throat– blue, violet, and Activity in 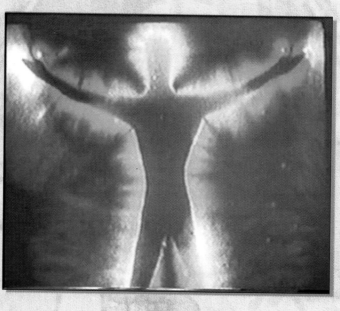 Hunt also Chakras carry the same mentioned in literature like Base root – Hypogastric/ orange, plexus – green, Third eye– Crown – white. certain

Journey through Chakras

Activity in certain charkas, seem to trigger increased activity in another. Dr. Hunt's measurements show definite frequencies for definite colours of the aura. All these measurements, along with all other measures of Human Energy Field, are consistent with normal physiological processes of the body and go beyond them to provide a vehicle for psychosomatic functioning.

Robert O. Becker, MD documented the human body energy as electrical frequency in his book called "The Body Electric". Bruce Tainio of Tainio Technology in Cheney, Washington developed an equipment to measure the bio frequency of human beings and foods, he used bio frequency monitors to determine the relationship

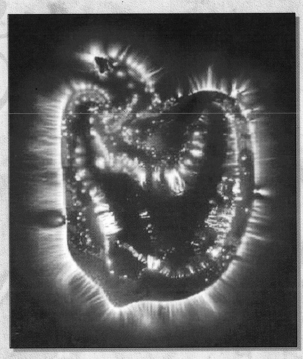

between frequency and disease. Measuring in megahertz, it was found that a healthy body typically has a frequency ranging from 62 to 78 MHz. As created all forms are perfect but whenever any imbalance occurs in the energy field it eventually shows up at the gross level too. The same way it has been observed that the process of disease sets in at 58 MHZ. This energy level can be disturbed even by a single negative thought. It was observed in various studies that negative thoughts lowered the measured frequency of a person up to 12 MHz and positive thoughts raised the measured frequency by 10 MHz. It was also found that prayer and meditation increased the measured frequency levels by 15 MHz. This gives credence to the fact that prolonged levels of stress, anxiety, depression etc. do result in lowering the body energy, as well as immune levels, allowing the disease to set in, as in case of all psycho somatic disorders.

TANTRA VISION

KUNDALINI "the biological basis of the genius" Gopi Krishna,

Right from the beginning of creation mankind has witnessed many transcendental

happenings represented in a child supernatural, psychic or intuitive mind or making true predictions are all different in our capabilities inspiring poems, some could could create beautiful awesome powers, others had course of investigation man within every individual energy, which is dormant some and fully Originally man energy after Goddesses, Divine will, later PRANA or SHAKTI, which called

genius, people with various powers as reading some ones or doing miracle healings. We some people could write highly create beautiful music, some paintings while some had awesome intellect. In the came to understand that there is a special form of in most, evolving in awakened in few. named this Gods, Angels and he discovered PRANA in Tantra is KUNDALINI.

TANTRA is religion nor sensory instant fulfillment of

neither a indulgence in gratifications for one's cravings and

desires. The word "TANTRA" comprises of two words TAN- 'Tanoti' meaning expansion and TRA-'Trayati' meaning liberation. Yoga and Tantra, work together, hand in hand, they lay down a complete system of practical understanding of human beings, while Tantra supplies the philosophy, yoga supplies the techniques of validation of the same, however everything in the field of spirituality is experiential thus subjective, as the experience of one may be similar but different than the other. According to Tantra, the range of mental experience can be broadened with the help of the senses. Your mind can have an experience based on an object within the framework of time and space or even beyond the framework of time, space and object. The later form of experience is the result of expansion of mind, beyond its defined boundaries and when it occurs there is a release of energy, within you. This latent energy within you is – KUNDALINI. Ancient Sages, Yogis and Tantriks have realized this dynamic potential force in the material body called KUNDALINI, which is the essential conscious power motivating all life functions and manifesting in personal development, non ordinary states and spiritual transformation.

Gopi Krishna* described Kundalini as a biological mechanism, present in every human being, according to him the human cerebrospinal system is capable of a new amazing activity that is still unknown to science. It can be accelerated though the discipline of Yoga or through other religious exercises. The practice of meditation, carried on in the proper way regularly for a sufficient duration of time, tends to force a normally silent region in the brain to an astonishing activity. The idea that under the direct influence of the Cosmic Life Energy the human brain is still in a state of organic evolution, this fact is so important that, compared to it, all other discoveries of modern science pale into insignificance.

The term Kundalini comes from Sanskrit word kundal meaning coil. It is represented as three and a half coiled serpent, with its tail in the mouth. The comparison between a serpent and Kundalini comes from the nature of its movement, which is spiraling and serpent like. The three coils represent three gunas– tamas, rajas and sattava, or three states of consciousness waking, sleeping and dreaming relating to three types of experiences subjective, sensual (objective) and no experience. While the half coiled tail in mouth is represented as 'ego'. Till the time human consciousness is stuck in mundane that is, the material desires and needs, this energy is static. Once we go beyond our material needs and desires, and realize that there is a higher purpose in life, withdraw from our attachments and indulgences, only then we realize that there is another state of consciousness beyond normal waking, sleeping or dreaming state. At this time this static energy becomes kinetic and adopts a course upwards passing through various psychic centers called Charkas towards the seat of supreme consciousness, at the highest Seventh Chakra.

The experience of kundalini does not belong to physical body, though it is connected to it, nor it can identify with mental or astral body since its actual abode is causal body, where the concept of time, space and object are completely lost. This primal energy is considered to arise from the unconscious state, in the Mooladhar charka, which then passes through different phases and becomes one with the cosmic awareness in the highest realm of existence ie Sahasrara Chakra. kundalini awakning is an evolutionary process taking entire human race to higher level of consciousness.

When Kundalini gets activated, suddenly in Muladhar Chakra, it may not rise immediately, it may wake up and sleep again many times over like a child needs to be woken up a few times since he goes back to sleep again. Sometimes it even ascends to Swadhisthan or Manipura Chakra only to return back to Muladhar to sleep again. However, once the kundalini crosses the Astral bridge, at Manipura Chakra there is no going back. Stagnation in a chakra occurs whenever there is an obstruction either at one of the charkas or in Shushumna. Kundalini can remain in one of the charkas for many years or even a lifetime. Sometimes this blockage of the kundalini at a Chakra may result, in the person, realizing certain psychic powers (Sidhhis) associated with that Chakra. However, instead of realizing that the one is on the road and need to clear the blocks for further ascension the one tends to display these powers, nurturing their ego and causing further blocks. Manifestation of psychic powers (Sidhhi) related to a particular chakra is an indication that the one has evolved to that Chakra, however in some people these psychic powers (Siddhis) do not stay long or fade away as the Kundalini moves upwards quickly. Psychic powers often linger long only when kundalini is blocked in a Chakra. One may think that he is using these psychic powers for the good of the humanity, but this only feeds the ego, hindering further progress.

We are all at different levels of evolution, though Kundalini awakening process begins from Muladhar Chakra; it is not necessary that it happens the same way in all of us. Depending upon the level of evolution attained through spiritual practices (Sadhana) in your past life or through your parents spiritual practices or both, your Kundalini may begin ascension from higher Chakra for example Manipura Chakra, as you might be born with Kundalini already in Manipura Chakra. Since you can't remember your previous life, the same way you also don't have realization about the state of your kunadlini. There are many children born with awakened Kundalini and as they grow up they show different manifestations as being a great musician, artist, scientist, philosopher, poet, healer or even a prophet.

Awakening of Kundalini and its ascension through charkas is important for the evolution of mankind, since our present state of mind is not capable of handling all aspects of life. Our relationships with people, the love and the hatred, are the consequences of our mental state. Our agonies, pains, frustrations are not much due to life circumstances but more to our mental response. As Patanjali has mentioned in his Yoga sutras all pains and sufferings arise out of the modification of mind, which leads to our attachments (to people and things), possessiveness, jealousy, self centeredness etc. During the process of awakening of Kundalini, mind automatically stabilizes, the world remains the same but your perception of the world changes, resulting in the change of values in life, improving the quality of love and relationships, enabling you to balance out the disappointments and frustrations in life.

Kundalini yoga, considers this physical body as the basis which is not abstract, it considers that the supreme consciousness represents the highest possible manifestation of physical matter in this body. The matter of this physical body is being transformed into subtle forces- such as feelings, thinking, reasoning, remembering, postulating and doubting, in the gradual process of evolution, this psychic; supra sensory or transcendental power in man is the ultimate point in human evolution. However it will happen only if, you are destined. kundalini experience considered from the view point of individual transformation is said to be a path of enlightenment. However, if a large number of enlightened people were to appear in society, the result would have been a transformed society. The concept of Kundalini has so much of mysticism about it, that every body who knows even little about it, wants his kundalini to be awakened. However, kundalini awakening cannot be the sole objective of any spiritual practice it, in fact, it is the byproduct of

SUBTLE BODY & CHAKRAS

As per Kundalini Tantra, the human body is composed of three layers (bodies), which function as the vehicle for the inner self. These are not bodies in physical sense, rather a kind of energy sheath or vibratory field, which embodies the underlying consciousness. The physical body originates in the sexual union of the parents, this body we normally experience and sustain with food. Our awareness within this body constitutes the waking state of consciousness. It is made up of sixteen components– five sensory organs, five organs of action, five elements and the mind. The energetic basis or pure form of the physical body is subtle or astral body, represented as our AURA. The subtle body is also composed of sixteen components. Within the subtle body exist the seven major Chakras, which get fully activated with the force of Kundalini Shakti. However there is a more subtle body called causal body (Karan sharira), it is the cause of creative force behind the other two. In fact causal body is a HIGHER MIND and it is shaped like an egg around the other two bodies. These bodies are linked with one another through the charkas or energy centers.

These Charkas are like a centrally placed electricity pole from which electrical wires run to different places, lighting streets and houses in the vicinity. This arrangement is the same for each of the charkas. The nadis (conduits of pranas in the subtle body) pass through each chakra carry prana in both directions. There is a forward and backward pranic motion in the nadis, analogous to the flow of alternating current in electrical wires. The outgoing communication and the incoming reactions, enter and leave the charkas in the form of this pranic flow in the corresponding nadis. In a way, charkas are centers of interchange between physical, physiological and psychological energy within the physical dimension.

There are six charkas in the human body, directly connected to the higher un illuminated centers of the brain while the seventh is the highest center in the brain, the final culmination of kundalini shakti. Every form, every sound and every subtle colour, has a frequency that affects us, at physical, mental and emotional level and affect our charkas, in the same way our thought process affects them. Chakras open and close according to our emotions and our state of mind as the charkas are transfer points for our thoughts, emotions and physical functioning of specific endocrine glands. When we are balanced and acquire self–discipline our charkas

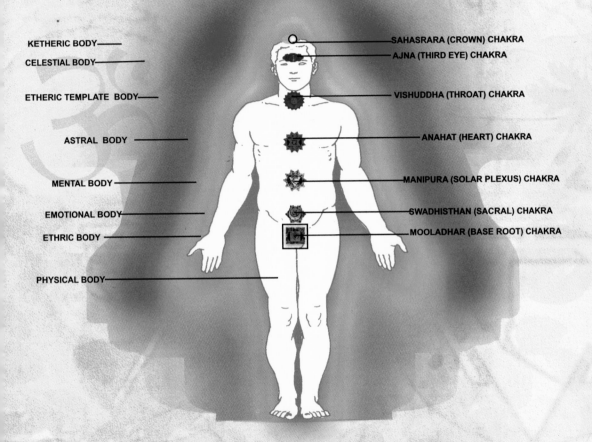

KETHERIC BODY———— SAHASRARA (CROWN) CHAKRA

CELESTIAL BODY———— AJNA (THIRD EYE) CHAKRA

ETHERIC TEMPLATE BODY———— VISHUDDHA (THROAT) CHAKRA

ASTRAL BODY ———— ANAHAT (HEART) CHAKRA

MENTAL BODY———— MANIPURA (SOLAR PLEXUS) CHAKRA

EMOTIONAL BODY———— SWADHISTHAN (SACRAL) CHAKRA

ETHRIC BODY ———— MOOLADHAR (BASE ROOT) CHAKRA

PHYSICAL BODY————

SUBTLE BODIES & CHAKRAS

pulsate with light, when our emotions are blocked they become dull and sluggish. These, in practice, are the ones responsible for the spiritual evolution of the 'being' through harmonious health of body, mind and spirit.

To understand Chakras and their effects fully it is important to understand all aspects related to them, the following chapters describe various Chakra attributes to facilitate understanding the subject better.

Three Gunas

Tantric texts and Ayuerveda the ancient Indian wisdom of health and healing, describe three prime attributes of Prakruti (Nature) called Gunas. These gunas are comparable to the three states of matter viz. solid, liquid and gaseous.

TAMAS- Is represented as principle of grossness, inertia, darkness, dullness and resistance. Tamas obscures truth behind illusion.

RAJAS- Is the principle of activity represents energy, movement, turbulence, power and desire. Rajas represents activity causes manifestations.

SATTVA- Is the principle of sublimation represents light, truth, perception, intelligence and harmony. Sattva is light in nature.

In both Sattva and tamas, a man abandons the world of senses. But in sattva he merges into light, while in tamas he merges into darkness.

The three gunas are compared to three states, of water, in solid state it is ice represents solidity, grossness, inertia and immobility termed as Tamasic. When this ice starts melting, like snow melting into water, it is active, free flowing described as Rajasic. With further rise in the heat, it starts evaporating as steam, leaving all the impurities behind, this process of sublimation of energy is termed as Sattva.

All the three gunas, are present in all of us. Gunas never become separated from each other, when one guna dominates the other two become recessive, like a three coloured strands braided together, sometimes one colour appears most dominant on the surface and sometimes others. All three are always present, but one sometimes hide the other from the view. When sattva dominates, rajas and tamas are pushed into background; at that time all desires, attachments, confusion, ignorance disappear, all that remains is light and bliss. When rajas dominates, it pushes sattva and tamas into background. There is a great rush of energy and a strong will to undertake work, projects and activities. And when tamas dominates,

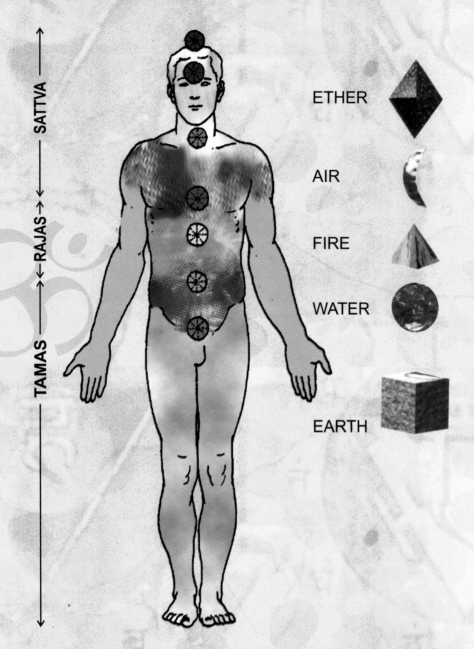

SATTVA

RAJAS

TAMAS

ETHER

AIR

FIRE

WATER

EARTH

PLACEMENT OF THREE GUNAS & FIVE ELEMENTS

rajas and sattva are in recess making the person ignorant, lazy and attached to material things. All three gunas depend on each other and help each other in the process of evolution and self development, the gross evolves back towards the subtle. In the process of bringing each other out, one guna serves as the stepping stone for another. A thing that is stable and tamas dominated is provided motivation and activity by rajas, that motion and activity helps in the process of realization as the thing moves to attain its true and essential nature– which is light– sattva.

Man is an evolute of the Universe, consciousness brought down and attached to material form. The natural flow of evolution is from subtle to gross. Ideas exist, first in the minds of men, then comes activity, starting a downward flow of energy. This downward flow continues, until energy gets entrapped in gross form. From sattva to rajas, to tamas, is the natural course of evolution, yet the same rajas can be used to convert tamas back into sattva. With his five sense organs and five organs of action man has the choice to either flow with gravity downwards to tamas or rise through activity upwards into light. This what all spiritual activities aim to achieve. To increase sattva one has to endure more pain as the tamas is consumed by the fire of self discipline. Once you understand the three gunas and their nature, you can recognize your level and assume responsibility for self development.

FIVE ELEMENTS (Panch Mahabhoot)

From the three gunas arise five elements–
From Sattva consisting of clarity comes the element ETHER (Space or Akash), from Rajas consisting of energy comes FIRE and from Tamas consisting of inertia comes EARTH. Between Sattava and Rajas arises, the subtle but mobile element AIR and between Rajas and Tamas, arises water combining mobility and inertia.

The five elements again represent the finer qualities of matter– solid, liquid, radiant, gaseous and ethereal. They delineate the five densities of all substances, all visible or invisible matter in the universe. These five elements constitute a continuum of energy from its densest, grossest vibrational level to the most subtle. At its lowest level, vibrational energy has substance (solidity), here the atoms are packed in compact, cohesive formed hence called dense and gross. It is termed as EARTH element or PRITHVI tattwa.

When excited to a higher frequency, the earth element loses the property of solidity. In this stage the energy is less dense– the atoms more dispersed allowing a higher frequency rate, the substance, hence becomes liquid and flowing. The liquid retains the property of form (of the holding vessel) and at this level of activity it is termed as WATER element (Jal Tattva).

As the level of vibrations increase, heat and light are generated by the accelerated motion. In this state the matter is less cohesive. Energy in this form is termed FIRE (agni). As the speed of individual particles continues to accelerate, all forms are lost, heat and light are no longer produced here all the semblance of cohesiveness of matter is lost. It is thus termed as AIR (Vayu ttatva).

 Finally, when the matter has lost all tactile qualities and is perceptible to human organism only as sound, it has attained the subtle most vibration called ETHER (akash ttatva). Here the individual particles of the matter no longer exists, but have vibrated beyond the material plane.

According to Ayurveda, the human body is composed of these same five elements. All elements have psychological correspondences that indicate states of mind and qualities of emotions. Accordingly these elements are also attributed to our charkas. We draw energy from all these five elements present in nature.

Our physical or gross body is the representation of earth element, which is represented and sustained by all the food we eat, which ultimately gets converted into nourishment for the entire physical body. As our base root Chakra is responsible for the gross/ physical body, earth element is attributed to this Chakra.

Our body, like this universe is composed of two third (2/3) water (fluids). Water is also one of the basic necessities. Water element also controls our emotional state and attributed to our Sacral or Swadhisthan Chakra which represents our emotional body.

The Fire (Agni) element in our body is represented as the body temperature, bhoot agni (mental fire), Jathar Agni (Digestive fire). In the same way Solar energy represents and nourishes our body's fire element and nourishes the body with vitamin D. Our Solar plexus or Manipura Chakra is attributed with fire element.

Air Element is represented in our body, through each of the breath we take, each breath not only provides us with the vital air, but also sustains us with the cosmic energy ie prana. This element is attributed to our heart or Anahat Chakra.

And last but not the least, is Space –most vital amongst all the five elements, as with out space no movement is possible, no circulation is possible in the body, everything will become so gross that life cannot survive. This element is attributed to our Throat or Vishhudhi Chakra.

GUNAS

ELEMENTS & ASSOCIATED SENSE

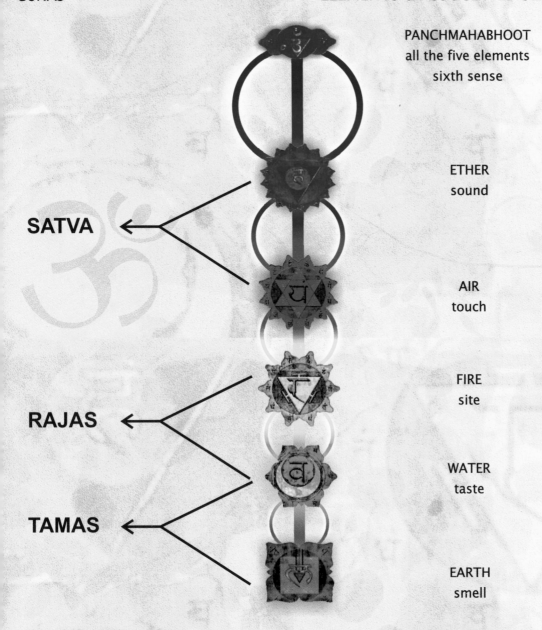

PANCHMAHABHOOT
all the five elements
sixth sense

ETHER
sound

SATVA

AIR
touch

FIRE
site

RAJAS

WATER
taste

TAMAS

EARTH
smell

We may survive without food for about 21 days, without water only a few days, without fire (ie even represented in our body temperature) few hours, without air few minutes and without space we are just gross– dead. In Ayurveda the balance of these prime elements is considered basic tenet of good health.

NADIS

"the subtle channels of consciousness"

The physical body has four main systems of distributing the pranas or energy-

The **circulatory system**-comprising of arterial/ venous and lymphatic systems.

The **nervous system**-including central, sympathetic and parasympathetic nervous systems.

The **endocrine system**- comprising of various ductless glands which regulate various aspects and functioning of the physical body through the secretion of hormones.

The **nadis**-the conduits of energy in subtle body.

'Nadi', comes from Sanskrit root word nad, meaning movement, as per Rigveda (ancient hindu scripture) it means stream, however the literal meaning of nadi is 'flow'. In gross or physical body we have various streams like arteries, veins, nerves, lymphatics as part of our circulatory system, in the same way the subtle body consists of various channel systems called Nadis. They are not nerves, but channels for the flow of consciousness, like negative and positive energy flows through a complex circuit, the same ways consciousness flows in the body through nadis. It is said that the ego or ahmkara does not reside in the physical body, but in subtle body and moves in the nadis, the ethereal nerves. When awakened, the dormant energy (kundalini) works through nadis.

According to tantric texts and Shiva Svarodaya, there are 72000 nadis (channels) in our body which are the conduits of pranas. Of these seventy two thousand nadis ten are significant, of which, three are the most significant forming the basis of Kundalini Tantra. These three nadis are called IDA (Left or Lunar Nadi) representing

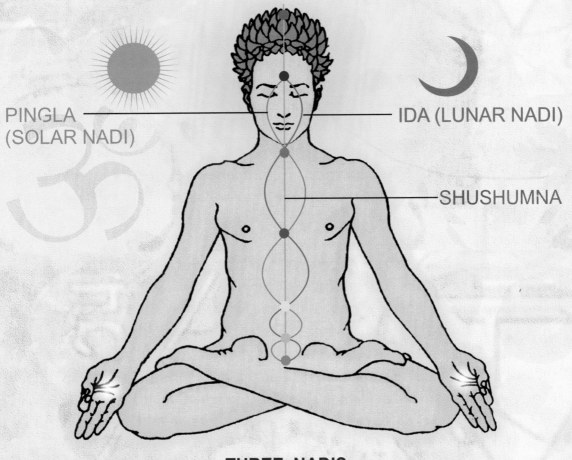

THREE NADIS

the cooling energy of moon, PINGALA (Right or Solar Nadi) representing the heating energy of Sun and SUSHUMANA which is closely associated with the spine and spinal cord at the subtle level.

It is said that the Sushumna runs through the center of the astral spine and corresponds to spinal canal, in the physical body and the charkas are strung upon it like lotuses. If you calculate as per numerology 7+2 =9, it represents the nine doors or pathways in our, through which the pranas can enter or leave our body.

These Nine doors arebasically our sense organs—two eyes, two nostrils, two ears, the mouth, the anus and the genitals. Most of the nadis begin or terminate on these doors. However, Sushumna is the most important nadi joining at the Crown chakra or fontelle at the physical body.

The control of these nadis enables you to control the ego, the mind and the senses, as the pranas moving with the breath, enkindles the body fire and carried to the mind which experiences the world through these doors. In Indian mythological texts Lord Krishna is attributed to have thousands of wives. According to the story, these women were the captives of a tyrant king, who was killed by Lord Krishna and got them released from the captivity. Then arose, the question of them being accepted by the society and so to give them acceptance in the society he declared all of them to be his wives. However, in spiritual sense a wife is attributed as a husband's desire and it is said that any one who can control all his desires would be KRISHNA.

Nadis are the channels of energy, which moves through each and every body part. They are the subtle counterpart of the physical flows, such as nervous energy and blood. They are not described in terms of structures but described as the conduits of Prana. Ida (Lunar nadi) considered as conscious and knowing, while and Pingla (Solar nadi) is vital and life giving; they are roughly translated as mind and body. As we discuss the polarization of the individual, mind and body, themselves are polarized, but complementary to each other. Ida represents moons energy and pingala as suns energy. Sushumna is supreme, it represents, the spirit or consciousness, it is the channel for the prana Shakti and the awakening of spiritual consciousness.

There are two basic systems in the body that control this Ida and Pingala and if we stimulate any component of one system, we turn on the whole system. Swar yoga the complete system of breath work emphasizes this aspect and this is how yoga asanas, pranayam, meditation and other yoga techniques affect the nadis and our health.

The ancient discipline of Swar Yoga (yoga of breath or unification through breath) describes that the nature of consciousness changes according to the dominance of one nostril over the other. If you observe your breathing pattern, it may be noticed that at any given time, the breath does not come in equal volume through both of our nostrils except for a brief period. Most of the time one nostril is more active than other and this dominance alternates, between left and right nostrils, in a regular pattern. Left nostril is associated with IDA nadi which culminates in the right hemisphere of brain, while the right nostril is associated with PINGALA nadi which culminates in the left hemisphere of the brain. The movement of energy, through these nadis, from one hemisphere to the other happens simultaneously with the change of breath from one nostril to the other. Therefore, when right nostril dominates, Pingala is active and left hemisphere dominates. In the same way when left nostril dominates, Ida is active and right hemisphere dominates. When both nostrils operate, both hemispheres operate in unison. When energy concentrates in the left hemisphere representing solar energy, one becomes more active, verbal, intellectual, extroverted, ambitious, creative and masculine. Conversely, right hemisphere dominance represents lunar energy and characterized with femininity, passivity, introversion, emotional responses and orientation to sight and sound. Human feelings are the by product of body chemistry and changing the breath pattern can change body chemistry.

The most significant of the nadis is Sushumna, which runs through the center of the astral spine and corresponds to the spinal canal in the physical body. It is like a high tension power line of the body, which extends unbroken from Sahasrara to the site of Kundalini, at Muladhar Chakra. Ida, Pingla and Susumna nadis begin in Muladhar Chakra in the pelvic floor, from where Sushumna flows directly upwards within the central canal, while ida passes to the left and pingla to the right, criss crossing each other at each higher charka. Susumna flows inside the central canal of the spinal cord while ida and pingla simultaneously flow on the outer surface of spinal cord, still within the bony vertebral column. In human physiology, two nadis roughly correspond with the two halves of the autonomic nervous system – the sympathetic and parasympathetic. Pingla coincides with the sympathetic nerves, responsible for stimulation and acceleration of activities concerning the external environment and deceleration of the organs, which tend to utilize a lot of energy internally. The sympathetic nerves speed up the heart, dilate the blood vessels, increase respiration rate and intensify the efficiency of eyes and ears etc.

The parasympathetic nerves directly oppose the sympathetic nerves, for they reduce the heartbeat, constrict the blood vessels and slow the breathing rate so that the person becomes introvert. The flow of prana in ida and pingla is completely involuntary, Basically, the Pingala represents the components of action and Ida represents the reception. Ida nadi controls all the mental process, while pingala nadi controls all the vital processes.

Ida is the energy within the personality, which is passive, receptive, feminine, negative, yin. At the physical level, it is dark, cold, lunar, energy dissipating, entropic, expansive (centrifugal) and relaxing. At mental level it is emotional, feeling, intuitive and non-discriminative, this is the soma psychic aspect of man, where energy is inwardly directed and body acts on mind. Ida controls the sense organs or Gyanendriyas (feeling centers), therefore give us the awareness and the knowledge of the world we live in.

Pingala can be defined as masculine, dynamic, active, positive, yang energy within our personality. It has a physical and mental side, represents light, heat, solar energy, creative, organizing, focused (centripetal) and contractive. It can be called psychosomatic energy, directed outward, directing organs of action (karmaendriyas), like mind acting on body. It is the basic life giving energy.

Kundalini awakening is awakening into awareness of the energy which can be used to heal, transform, energize and evolve higher level of consciousness. The whole science of Kundalini yoga concerns the awakening of Sushumna; once Sushumna comes to life, a means of communication between the higher and lower dimensions of consciousness is established and the awakening of kundalini occurs. Shakti travels up to Sushumna, to become one with Shiva in Sahasrara and the entire store of energy in man is unleashed.

THREE GRANTHIS

Ida, Pingla and Sushumna arise from Mooladhar, in the pelvic floor while Sushumna flows directly upwards within the central canal, ida passes to the left and pingla to the right, criss crossing at each higher charka. At the point of crossing over at Mooladhar, Heart and third eye Chakra are what Tantric scriptures mention, about three granthis (psychic knots) in physical body. These granthis (knots) are basically three levels of awareness, we have to move through in the process of kundalini awakening and spiritual progress. Named after the three deities (Trinity) Brahma (the creator), Vishnu (the sustainer) and Rudra (or Shiva/Mahesh –the dissolutor), these granthis pose as obstacles and each aspirant or the seeker has to cross these barriers on the path of Kundalini awakening and spiritual progress.

Brahma Granthi is located in the region of Mooladhar, the first Chakra and is the first point of cross over, in the path of kundalini awakening. Though some tantric scriptures place Brahma granthi in the region of naval, as it is also considered, the knot of the samsara (the world of name and forms). Since the first charka refers to physical survival it implies to our attachment to material things, physical pleasures and self–centeredness– the world of Maya. Till the time we stay embedded in tamas (gross world) our mind is trapped, we are ignorant to the reality and experience ego-centric ness, lethargy and negativity. This knot is the major obstacle in the spiritual path, creates a lot of restlessness and distraction of the mind. To overcome the obstacles associated with Brahma Granthi an aspirant has to go beyond the senses and sensory pleasures, rise beyond tamas. Once the energy becomes pure and radiant the knot can be untied and frees the aspirant from the bondages of attachments and selfishness.

Vishnu Granthi is the next level of cross over located at the heart charka. It is associated with the bondages created by our attachments, especially emotional attachments to people and things. Patanjali, in his Yoga Sutras has mentioned attachments as a source of pain and sufferings. Heart Chakra is associated with devotion, love and faith, in a detached manner, attachment to these traits is the imbalance of the heart Chakra. For example, there is a little difference between empathy and sympathy. While empathy is a balanced state and sympathy is an imbalance and works as a block in our spiritual progress. Therefore, only by

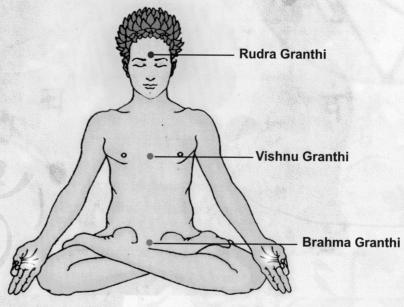

Rudra Granthi

Vishnu Granthi

Brahma Granthi

PLACEMENT OF THREE GRANTHIES (PSYCHIC KNOTS)

"Vivek"– absolute discrimination, knowledge and faith, one can untie this knot.

In ancient India spiritual aspirant used to give up the family life (Griasth Ashram) and undertake asceticism (Sannyas Ashram) by giving up worldly living and home thereby allowing them to free themselves from deep ties of attachment in a family tree and even going beyond the genetic code. This process is done with all rituals and even funeral rites of the person are performed to complete the process of disconnection of ties. These people are called "divij"– twice born, now again for spiritual purpose only.

Rudra Granthi is located in the area of Third Eye Chakra. Rudra is the principle of dissolution and when the untying of this knot happens, only then the duality ends and the aspirant's Ego is dissolved. This Granthi is also associated with attachment to siddhis and psychic powers, feeding to our ego. This is the point of transcendence wherein time bound consciousness gets dissolved and the yogi establishes himself into infinity by ascending himself, to the Crown Chakra, to experience total bliss.

FIVE ENERGETICS (VAYU)

Medical science describes two types of nervous systems, in addition to sympathetic and parasympathetic which are sensory or information system and motor system. According to Tantra, we have two types of energy reaching every organ of the body. One is known as Prana Shakti or the vital/ dynamic energy and another is Manas shakti or the mental energy. Pathway of the pranic flow in the body are nadis (channels of energy) which are different than the nerves, since nerves are part of physical body, the nadis are the part of subtle body.

When we talk of prana we are talking of the vital life force not the breath, air or oxygen. The vital energy has five variants for different functions in the body not as different manifestations. These five variants, in Ayurveda and Tantra, are called Vayu (Energy) which moves through various nadis and have different functions and are represented at basic five charkas.

- PRANA Vayu– Its not the overall prana or vital energy, but the energy or Prana represented between the larynx and the top of the diaphragm, represented at the heart charka. It governs the functions of heart and lungs besides all other activities in that region of heart charka from breathing to swallowing and blood circulation.

- APANA Vayu– Centered in the pelvic region between the navel and perineum and represented at Muladhar Chakra, it regulates all the excretory functions and responsible for the expulsion of gas, wind, faeces, urine and even foetus at the time of birth. Its movement is downwards.

- VYAN Vayu– Though represented at the Sacral or Swadhisthan Chakra, this vital force pervades the whole body and governs circulatory system and movement of joints and muscles.

- SAMANA Vayu– Word Saman means equal or balanced, this Vayu centered in small intestine between naval and rib cage provides balance between two opposite energies Apana and Prana Vayu. Samana is represented at Manipura

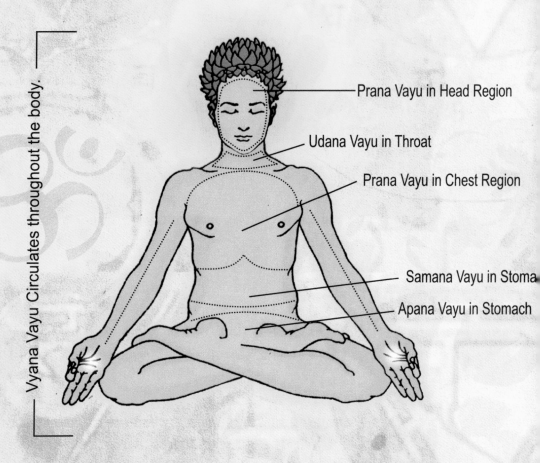

Prana Vayu in Head Region

Udana Vayu in Throat

Prana Vayu in Chest Region

Samana Vayu in Stoma

Apana Vayu in Stomach

Vyana Vayu Circulates throughout the body.

**PLACEMENT OF FIVE ENERGETICS (VAYU)
IN THE BODY**

- or Solar plexus charka, it activates and controls the digestive organs and their secretions.

- UDANA Vayu– Centered in throat it controls sympathetic and parasympathetic nervous system and communication of all kinds, will, memory and exhalation.

ANATOMICAL & PHYSIOLOGICAL ASPECTS

Our chakras are associated with various organs and glands. The impact of yogic and spiritual practices involves nervous system and the charkas are said to be present at the points of nerve plexues. There has been a section of people of scientific and yogic mind, sought to understand and explain the physical and psychic aspects of kundalini and charkas. Dr. J.K. Sarkar, in his paper titled "Anatomical and physiological basis of Raja Yoga" had tried to explain the working of charkas through nervous and endocrine system.

Human nervous system is composed of two parts– the central (or somatic) nervous system CNS), responsible for voluntary actions; and the autonomic nervous system (ANS) which is independent of our will.

The former involves brain and all its divisions within the skull (including the cerebral cortex, thalamus, hypothalamus, pituitary, pineal body etc; the mid brain, the cerebellum, the pons and the medulla oblongata) and whole length of spinal column. The CNS sends and receives nerve impulses to or from the entire body, and its periphery with the help of 43 pairs of nerves arising from the brain and spinal cord. The higher centers for thinking, hearing, seeing, movement etc. are located in the different areas of the cerebral cortex. The four ventricles or cavities of the brain and the narrow canal in the spinal cord contain a fluid called cerebrospinal fluid (CSF) in the form of a continuous stream.

The ANS controls the activities of the internal organs and consists of two divisions: the sympathetic and parasympathetic. The parasympathetic nerves arise from the brain, as well as from the lower part of the spinal cord. Their actions are usually localized, such as slowing of the heart etc. and help to conserve body energy. The sympathetic system consists of nerves arising from the middle part of the spinal cord and forming two long trunks on the two sides of the spine, extending from the base of the skull to the coccyx (a small triangular bone below the triangular sacrum).

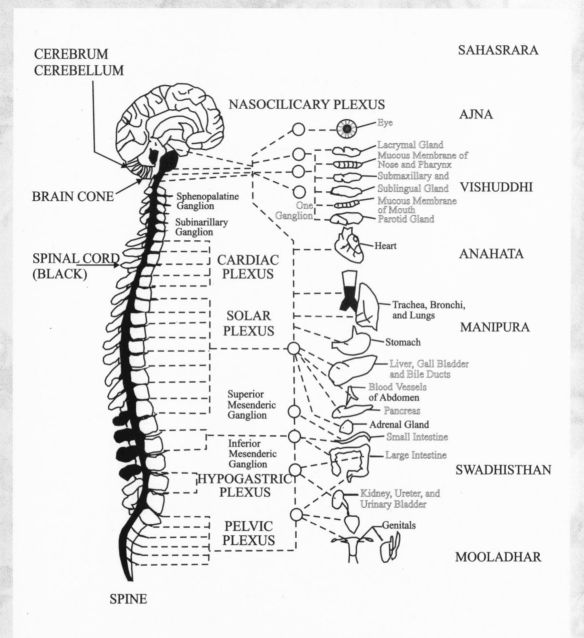

PHYSICAL ANATOMY AND
THE PSYCHIC CHAKRAS

The two sympathetic trunks contain several ganglions (congregation of nerve cells) meet terminally at a small ganglion called ganglion Impar, in front of coccyx. Sympathetic nerves arising from the ganglia on these two trunks form various nerve plexus (network of fine nerves) on their way to different body organs like uterus, intestine, heart etc. the reaction of sympathetic nerves are mass reactions like constriction of arteries, acceleration of heart rate, slowing of gastric movement. Though ANS is outside the CNS has certain control centers in the brain.

Sushumna is considered to be the central canal of the spinal cord, which is continuous above the cavities of the brain and thus in direct contact with the hypothalamus and pineal gland. The spinal cord lies only in the upper two-third of the vertebral column. In the lower third of the spine, it tapers off abruptly into a conical extremity. From the apex this conical extremity, a delicate non-nervous filament named Filum Terminale, descends to the coccyx, the lowest bone of the vertebral column. The lower part of the Filum Terminale is in the vicinity of the inferior hypogastric plexus. There are various other autonomic nerve plexus, situated on the two sides of the vertebral column conceived and associated as the lotuses of various charkas. Suggested anatomical site for these lotuses are as under–

- Mooladhar or Base Root Chakra – Inferior Hypogastric Plexus (pelvic Pleexus)
- Swadhisthan (Sacral) Chakra – Superior hypogastric plexus.
- Manipura (Solar Plexus) Chakra– Coeliac or Solar Plexus
- Anahhat (Heart) Chakra– Cardiac Pleaxus
- Visudhha (Throat) Chakra – Plexuses connecting superior, middle and inferior cervical ganglia.
- Ajna (Third Eye) Chakra – Internal carotid plexus.
- Sahasrara– Pineal Body

ASSOCIATED ENDOCRINE GLANDS

Human body consists of two kinds of glands, one set is exocrine glands and another is endocrine glands. Exocrine glands are the glands which release their secretions through ducts like liver and gall bladder etc. while endocrine glands are ductless glands which release their secretions called hormones directly into the bloodstream and affect us physiologically, physically and psychologically. The hormones secreted by our endocrine glands are the chemical messengers and together with the autonomic nervous system they maintain parameters for optimum growth. Since nervous and endocrine system, are interconnected functionally, imbalance in one affects the other. The location of seven major chakras is approximately the same as of our endocrine glands and our chakras directly or indirectly regulate the functions of the endocrine glands. In the same way the imbalance of chakras affect our endocrine glands, manifesting in terms of physical symptoms. Some even believe that certain of the endocrine glands like thymus and pineal body are physically non existent, by the time we become adults and their functions are regulated by our chakras.

The Hypothalamus and Pituitary Gland–

The hypothalamus is a small region of the brain that activates and regulates the part of the nervous system that controls the involuntary body functions, the hormonal system and many other body functions such as regulating sleep, body temperature and appetite. It has complex interconnections with the cerebral cortex and the other parts of the brain, which are little understood, links emotions with the body's autonomic nervous system. It is regulated by our AJNA or Third Eye chakra.

The pituitary gland, a pea sized structure like an upside down mushroom, hangs by a stalk from the undersurface of the brain. This vital gland influences growth, metabolism and stimulates activities of other glands. By producing a range of controller hormones, it orchestrates the secretion of hormones from other endocrine glands like–Human Growth Hormone, F.S.H. (Follicle Stimulating Hormone), ACTH, Prolactin, Thyroid Stimulating Hormones (Vasopresin, Oxytocin)

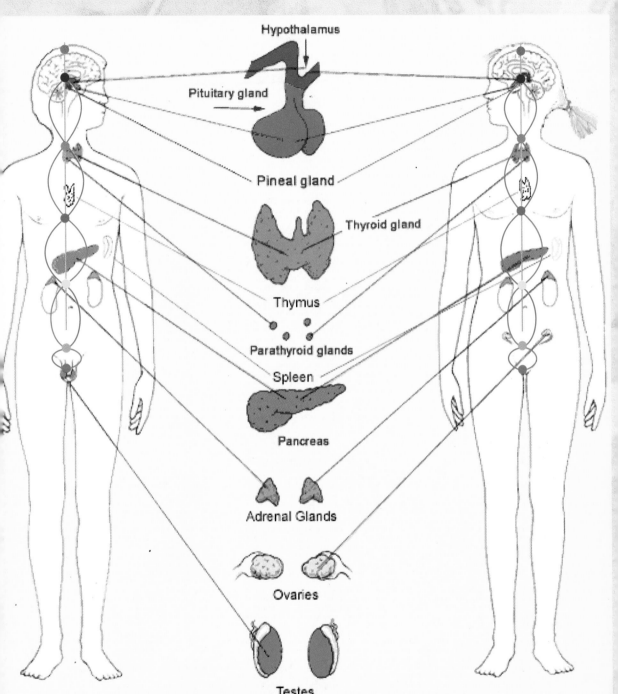

Hypothalamus

Pituitary gland

Pineal gland

Thyroid gland

Thymus

Parathyroid glands

Spleen

Pancreas

Adrenal Glands

Ovaries

Testes

Our Endocrine Glands

etc. Because, the hypothalamus controls the pituitary it indirectly masterminds its orchestration. That is why AJNA chakra is referred as Master or Guru chakra.

Pituitary gland has two lobes called anterior and posterior lobes and releases a wide range of different hormones including the ones responsible for contractions during child birth and the ones regulating and release of milk from breast for baby feeding. It is interesting to note that the intuition of nursing mother is at its peak, since the nursing as well as intuition, are associated to our third eye chakra.

Adrenal glands–

The adrenals attached on top of each of our kidneys, are associated to our Mooladhar or base root chakra. Each has two parts an outer cortex and an inner medulla.

In response to ACTH from pituitary, the cortex secretes a number of steroid hormones that directly affect the balance of salt, water and glucose in the body. cortisol normally secreted by the adrenal cortex, affects glucose metabolism, according to a daily sleep and wake cycle, as its concentration in the blood is much higher during the day than night. During a stress response, cortisol secretion rises in proportion to the degree of stress. This is more marked when the stress arises, from physical injury. cortisol increases the concentration of glucose in our body, by breaking down proteins, fats and carbohydrates. As a result, stress increases the level of blood sugar, an appropriate response to acute stress to ensure adequate energy supply, for both the brain and skeletal muscles at a time when immediate physical activity may be required.

Besides ACTH, the pituitary produces endorphins and other related compounds. The precise mode of operation of these compounds, is still not completely clear, however it is assumed that their pain relieving properties, along with other postulated effects on mood and perception, may combine to allow life saving exertion, despite serious injury. As in the case of many acts of heroism.

The adrenal medulla is intimately associated with the sympathetic nervous system. Its main secretion – adrenalin – is related to noradrenaline, one of the most important neuro transmitters of the sympathetic system. Adrenalin secretion is initiated by direct stimulation of the adrenal medulla by the sympathetic nerves.

Exposure to a stressor produces an immediate increase in sympathetic nerve activity, which in turn results in the release, into the blood stream, of significant quantities of adrenaline from the adrenal medulla, preparing the body for fight or flight situation. Once this hormone is released, in the blood, it can quickly permeate the tissues of the body, augmenting the activity of sympathetic nerves. The effects of this are well known- increased heart rate and breathing rate, palpitation, trembling, hair raising etc. Along with these predominant physical responses the feedback to the brain arouses the emotional response to stress, normally some degree of fearfulness and anxiety, therefore impacting Base root, Solar plexus and Heart chakra.

Thyroid Gland–

Thyroid is shaped like a butterfly or a bow tie and located across the front of the upper part of the trachea (windpipe) regulated by our Throat chakra. The cells of the thyroid manufacture hormones which are released into the blood stream in order to control the rate of metabolism (the process of oxygen uptake and subsequent production of energy and heat within the body) in all the other tissues and organs. While all other endocrine glands produce their secretions when required, the thyroid stores, within itself, around three months supply of its hormones. In most people thyroid production is controlled within fairly narrow limits but severe stress exposure, may result in increased production. Throat chakra related to self expression is easily affected by emotional stress and bottled emotions which may have direct or indirect effect on thyroid gland as well as Heart chakra.

The Pancreas–

Most of the pancreas is non- endocrine in nature, being concerned with producing digestive juices for the gut. Its function is regulated by our Solar plexus or Manipura chakra. Pancreas is situated behind the stomach, embedded within the bulk of its tissue lie numerous clusters of endocrine cells, called islets of langerhans, which secrete insulin and glucagon, two substances, with essentially complementary actions in the maintenance of normal glucose levels. Insulin lowers the blood sugar by encouraging the body cells to absorb more glucose, glucagon, on the other hand raises blood sugar levels by mobilizing the sizeable store of carbohydrates present in liver and converting it to glucose.

Gonads (Testes & Ovaries)–

Our Gonads are regulated by Base root as well as Sacral chakra, since testes and ovaries play an important role as hormone producing endocrine organs, in addition to producing sperm and egg cells. In both the sexes, the manufacture and release of sex hormones during reproductive life is controlled by the hypothalamus and pituitary, much the same way as they control other endocrine organs.

It is well accepted that both acute and chronic stress can affect the hormonal balance of the female reproductive system. Irregularities of the menstrual cycle and disturbance or inhibition of ovulation occur commonly in the presence of both physical and emotional stressors. These effects are the result of imbalances of hypothalamus and pituitary, since increased level of cortisol secretions have an inhibitory effect on the brain. Therefore it can be assumed, that as mental stress affects sexual function and Sacral chakra, same way emotional stress affects mental activity affecting Third eye or Ajna chakra.

Men are also affected by stress, leading to common sexual dysfunction such as difficulties with erection, premature ejaculation and sometimes affecting the sperm production.

Pineal Gland–

This small organ (6mmx4mm) lies deep within the brain appears about 36th day of gestation, gains maximum development at about 7 years and undergoes involution up to about 14 years. Vestiges of the gland are recognized recently and termed as pineal body, contains pinealocytes– a peculiar type of cells not found any where, It is considered a part of the brain but lacks in true nerve cells. It is outside the brain blood barrier and produces an enzyme, produced no where else in the body and necessary for the development and functioning of gonads, pituitary and thyroids. It is associated with our Crown chakra and secretes melatonin, which is important to maintain our sleep/ wake cycles and associated daily rhythms (such as cortisol secretion) in synchrony with the dark/ light cycle. The balance of this delicate rhythm is easily upset by events such as changing time zones, going on night duty and other causes of sleep disturbance.

Thymus Gland–

Thymus, regulated by our Heart Chakra though referred as a gland, however it is now accepted that the primary function of this gland is, a regulatory component of the immune system. It is most active before birth and during early life after which it becomes smaller. According to researchers despite its size in adult life, it continues to secrete significant volume of the hormone thymosin, to affect our immune level.

The thymus is responsible for the initiation and maintenance of an essential component of the immune response, underlying the importance of Heart chakra as responsible for the sustenance. It produces and programs T– cells (a type of white blood cells), which can distinguish between body's own protein and that of foreign origin such as invading germs and bacteria or genetically mutated cells. When the system identifies such foreign proteins it can mobilize the resources to destroy and remove them. Thymosin is involved in the maintenance of T cells function, malfunction or maldevelopment leads to overwhelming infection or the uncontrolled multiplication of mutated cells, which may manifest as cancer as well as AIDS.

The holistic approach to health fully acknowledges the integration of mind and body. The wellbeing of one depends on the good health of other.

CHARKA Location and attributes

Tantra and eastern yogic system describes seven major charkas between head and torso, corresponding to the major nerve plexuses in the body, while acknowledging varying numbers of minor chakras, all over the body. Chakras are like vortices of energy attached to Susumna nadi or the spine at the subtle level. Each major chakra on the front (ventral aspect)) of the body is having its counterpart on the back (dorsal aspect) of the body, which can be considered as the front or rear aspect of the chakra stated as vortices or openings. However the first ie Mooladhar and Seventh ie Crown chakra have one open ended points only and termed as single vortice chakras. From Sacral to Third Eye chakras are double vortice chakras, the ventral aspect is related to feelings and the dorsal aspect is related to will center. Since the ventral aspect associated to the feelings is considered highly sensitive, it is therefore recommended that in healing process only self healing is done on the front, while a healer can work from the back or dorsal side. It is also interesting to note that at the lower part of the body Mooladhar and Sacral chakras are connected at a "T" junction and same way at the top other end Third Eye and Crown chakras are connected at a "T" junction.

In tantric depiction of chakra symbology, we also find different aspects; each of these aspects has spiritual relevance if understood properly –

- Petals of the lotus flower
- Colour of the chakra
- the Yantra or geometrical shape
- the bija mantra
- the animal symbol
- the deities associated as higher and divine beings.

In Tantra and Yoga, charkas are depicted as Lotus flowers, each chakra is represented as various set of Lotus petals– four, eight, ten, twelve, sixteen, two and thousand petaled lotus from

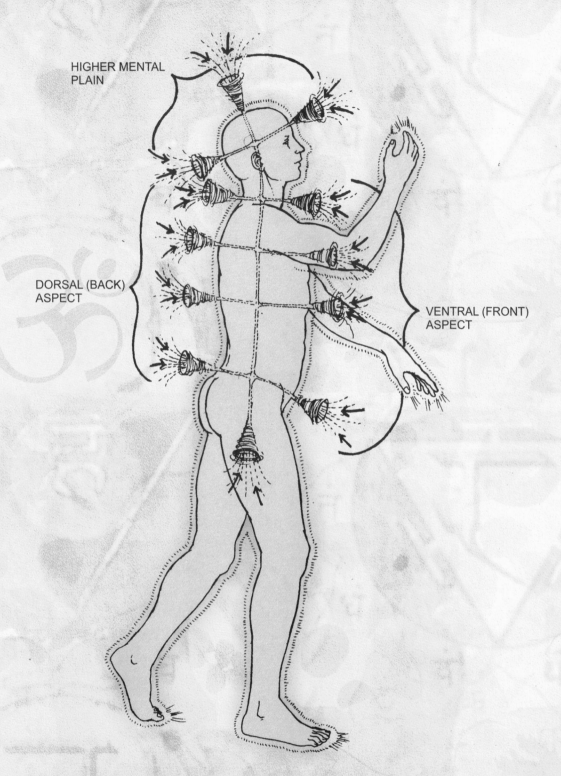

HIGHER MENTAL
PLAIN

DORSAL (BACK)
ASPECT

VENTRAL (FRONT)
ASPECT

VENTRAL (FRONT), DORSAL (BACK) ASPECTS
OF CHAKRAS AND CHAKRA VORTICES

Mooladhar to Crown chakra. In Indian spiritual system the Lotus flower is highly revered and used as the seat for most of the deities. The Lotus plant is used as an example of ascension, since the plant sprouts in mud, symbolizing Tamas and ignorance; grows through water symbolizing Rajas, endeavour and aspiration and eventually reaches the air and blooms under the direct light of the sun, symbolizing Sattva and illumination. Thus lotus symbolizes evolution of man from the lowest state of awareness, to the highest state of consciousness. The number of petals is represented as the nerve endings at each of the chakra plexus.

Ancient sage, thousands of years ago, envisioned the chakras as moving energy centers and assigned the colour and the number of petals accordingly. While Dr. Valorie Hunt and associates, in their research in 1988, measured chakras energy movement in Hertz or cycles per second and concluded that auric colours correlated with the same frequency wave pattern as in a rainbow. Their research showed colour / frequency correlations. These explained that these frequency bands, except for extra bands at blue and violet, are in reverse order of rainbow colour sequence, as assigned to the chakras. But different practitioners may visualize different colour sequence during meditation, which is also accepted true and correct.

The animals on the charka represent our previous evolution, besides the animals are also used as symbols of elements. Even in astrology animals are assigned to various zodiac signs, while entire Chinese astrology is based on animal symbols only. In chakra system animals are the objective representation of the respective chakra and symbolize the psychological meaning of the individual chakra; as the elephant in root or Mooladhar chakra represents stability and memory of previous births. Certain chakra healers suggest visualization of chakra related animals, as well as colour visualization.

Indian mythological scriptures are having a host of deities, which are assigned to various chakras. These deities represent our higher consciousness and ancient Indian sages used to prescribe prayers to certain deities as a way to balance the related or assigned chakra. Each of the chakra depicts a male deity and a female deity (a form of Shakti) besides a ruling deity like Ganesha, the elephant god, as the ruling deity of Mooladhar chakra. He is always prayed to, at the beginning of all rituals, to remove all obstacles in life and attain stability. Similarly there are depictions of various deities, at each of the other chakras, which are explained while discussing the respective chakra in detail.

BIJA MANTRA

The word Bija means seed, a Bija mantra is seed syllable which is the source of basic vibration of a mantra. In a verse of the mantra the vibrations arise mainly from these seed syllables. Each of the chakra is assigned a seed syllable like Lam, yam, Ram, Yam, Hum and Om from Mooladhar/ root chakra to Ajna/ Third Eye chakra. The sound of Om has two vibrations the first aspect in the beginning produces sound of "N" which can be prolonged as a nasal aspect when chanted and ending in "M" which marks the culmination, even the mouth closes.
Aa...uuuu.....nnnnnnnnnnnnnnnn...m.

So, the fist aspect of with "N" effect is associated with the Third Eye or Ajna chakra, while the later aspect with "M" effect is associated with Sahasrara or Crown chakra, where everything culminates in the place of total void.

These seed syllables when Chanted with focus on the chakra point, transfer your breath vibrations and energy to the respective chakra.
(For detailed guidance refer to the Chapter on chakra meditation).

OM (Au..n...m)
Sahasrara (Crown) Chakra
& Ajna (Third Eye)

Hu..m
Vishuddha (Throat) Chakra

Ya..m
Anahat (Heart) Chakra

Ra..m
Manipura (Solar Plexus) Chakra

Va..m
Swadhisthan (Sacral) Chakra

La..m
Mooladhar (Base Root) Chakra

Each of the chakra is depicted as various sets of lotus petals for example Mooladhar or base root chakra is depicted as four petalled lotus, Sawdhisthan chakra is depicted as six petalled lotus and so on. There is a Sanskrit letter on each of the petal of each of the chakra. Sanskrit language has fifty letters which are inscribed on each petal of the chakra from root to third eye chakra. So, the four last letters of the alphabet are inscribed on the four petals of the root chakra.

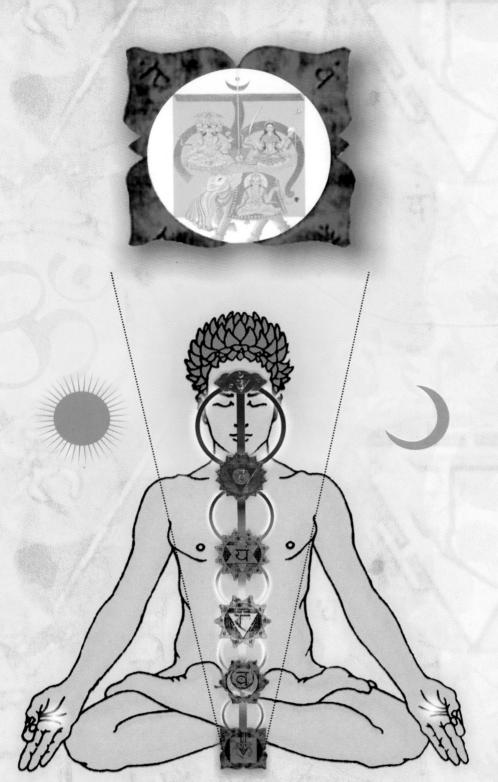

MOOLADHAR (BASE ROOT) CHAKRA

MOOLADHAR (BASE ROOT) CHAKRA

Guna : Tamasic
Principle Element : Earth
Vayu : Apana
Structural Representation : Four Petals
Colour : Crimson Red
Auric Layer– Physical / Etheric Body
Site : Pelvic floor and corresponds to coccygeal plexus
Sense Organ: Nose
Associated Sense: Smell
Work Organ: Anus
Corresponding Gland : Adrenal & Gonads
Main Issues– Survival/physical needs
Developmental age – 1–7 years
Vehicle of the Bija: Elephant with seven trunks
Associated Deity: Ganesha
Associated Planet: Mars
Associated Zodiac Sign: Capricorn
Related Essential Oils: Jatamansi (Indian Spikenard), Patchauli,
Valerian root, Nagarmotha, Lotus root, Costus root oils
Associated Crystals– Coral, Jasper,
Hematite & Black /brown /moss Agate

Traditionally, the subtle body or Aura is considered to be formed of seven layers, each corresponding and sequentially related to a definite charka. The first layer of the energy field the Etheric body (the etheric state between energy and matter) over our physical body is connected to our first charka called the MOOLADHAR or BASE ROOT CHAKRA. This layer is associated with automatic and autonomic functions of the body, as the Charka is associated with the physical functioning and physical sensation or feeling of pain and pleasure. Mooladhar is the first chakra in the spiritual evolution of man, where one goes beyond animal consciousness and starts to be a real human being.

Located between anus and genitals, area of pelvic plexus, this chakra represents the "grounding" of the being in the material world. It stands for the will to survive attitude. Positioned at the coccyx, it acts as the energy pump where in lies the dormant 'Kundalini' energy, representing physical potency and vitality in a person in whom it is active.

Muladhar charka represents a persons Mool Prakruti (basic nature) – the manifestation of the individual consciousness into human form. It is most active during the first seven years of a new born child and it is responsible for the physical development of the being, imbalance at that stage results in physical problems or deformity or insecurity in the child. A young child acts out of this first chakra motivation during the initial seven years and acts self centered and highly concerned with his or her physical survival and security. This is the phase an infant has to ground him/her self and establish the laws of his /her world, learning to regulate patterns of eating, drinking and sleeping, securing his/her worldly identity.

Mooladhar chakra is represented as a four petalled lotus of crimson red colour. In tantric scriptures it is mentioned that each of the petals having letters vam वं, sham षं, sham शं, sam सं, (last four letters of Sanskrit alphabets) written in gold. In the pericarp is a yellow square, the yantra symbol of earth element. This yellow square is supported by an elephant with seven trunks. Elephant, as an animal represents strength and solidity. The seven trunks of the elephant denote the seven minerals vital to physical functioning. It is also said that elephant has strong memory and the seven trunks represent memories of past seven lives, Mooladahr chakra also is having the imprints of our past lives or the tribe memory bank.

This chakra represents a person's grounding in this physical world, hence called the base root chakra, therefore it represents the element earth. This element is important for grounding of trees, same way earth is important for human beings to stay healthy and stable in life. Those who are unstable in life and are changing residences, jobs, relationships or having constant health problems need to work on their root chakra. Ancient sages were able to visualize chakras and suggested simple remedies to balance the chakra imbalances. As in case of weak base root chakra, they used to  prescribe daily visit, bare feet for a month, to a Peepal or Baniyan trees (both are renowned for their healthy roots), offer water and take seven parikrima (rounds) around the tree. Though, in earlier days a lot people thought of it as superstition, but logically, exposure to earth element during bare feet visits and the contact with strong roots, helped to remove chakra imbalances and strengthened root chakra, resulting into removal of obstacles from their lives. Obstacles are nothing but the imbalances, in our mind and body, even when we promote meditation, the basic purpose is to restore the balance of mind, body and the spirit.

Resting on top, of the inverted triangle is the bija mantra lam लं . Inside the bindu, over the mantra reside the elephant deity Ganesha and devi Dakini, who has four arms and bright red eyes and is the carrier of pure intelligence. Tantra, associates Ganesha, as the ruling deity of this chakra. Another name for Ganesha is Ganapati– while pati means nurturer, Gana is the guardian deity of eight vasus (directions). So Ganapati is the lord of all directions. Ganesha belongs to Shiva family, created by Parvati (Shiva's consort) out of mud and invoked life in it. As she wanted him to guard the entrance of the dwelling, while she had gone for her bath. During this period Shiva returns home but is not allowed to enter inside, since he was not known to Ganesha. Being not allowed entry, in his own home, angers Shiva who beheads the baby boy and enters the house. Later realizing, through Parvati, his mistake of beheading their son, he wanted to revive the boy but the head of the boy had disappeared; so he goes to the jungle (woods), beheads a baby elephant sleeping with his head towards north and places the head on the boy's shoulders and invokes prana (life) in him.

Some people say Kundalini resides in Mooladhar chakra while other believe it to reside in Sacral or Swadhisthan chakra, if you see chakra vortices (as explained earlier) the root chakra and sacral chakra together form a T junction at the tip of Sushumna. Our Mooladhar chakra is the first doorway of energy, whose deity is Ganesha, where Kundalini (Shakti or Parvati) resides. Therefore certain spiritual Guru's suggest prayers and chanting of Lord Ganesha to remove obstacles caused by root chakra imbalances.

The relevance of the baby elephant being beheaded while sleeping with head in north can be found in fundamental principles of Vastu, ancient Indian science of structures and living. Our head represents North Pole and feet represent South Pole. If we sleep with our head in north, similar poles cause disturbance of body's magnetic current affecting entire physiology and health. That is the reason ancient Indian scriptures describe north as the direction of death, for sleeping purpose; otherwise north is considered the direction of Kuber (lord of wealth).

This chakra is also associated with our sense of smell. Out of the five basic senses, the sense of smell is the primordial and the most basic. Mooladhar chakra is supposed to be the highest chakra in animals and the animals have a very well developed sense of smell. Even a new born recognizes his/her mother by her smell only.

The vayu or energetic associated with this chakra is Apan vayu, regulating the energy of elimination from body. Physiologically, this chakra is related to excretory, urinary, sexual and reproductive organs and influences, large intestine functions, bowel movement, regulates adrenals and gonads. Imbalance or blockages of the basic charka, produce physical complaints related to skeletal system, regenerative powers, irregular bowel movement, as well as the renal system problems; resulting into the following symptoms like brittle bones, slowed recovery even from common ailments, frequent illness, accident proneness, arthritis, skin disorders, constipation, fistula, fissures and hemorrhoids etc. Some other related diseases are cancer, leukemia, sexual ailments, allergy as well as growth and psychological problems.

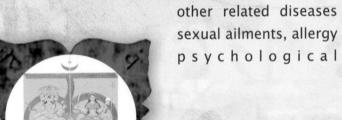

Jaspers

Hematite

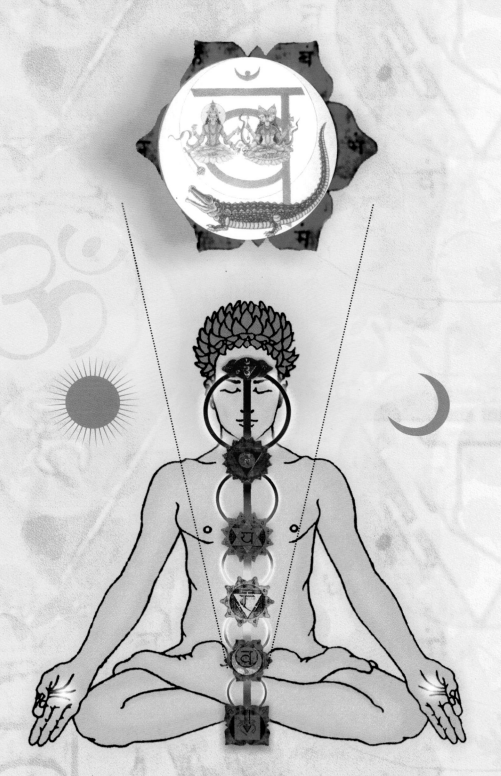

SWADHISTHAN (SACRAL) CHAKRA

SWADHISTHAN (SACRAL or SEXUAL) chakra

Guna: Rajasic.

Principle element: Water.

Vayu: Vyana.

Structural representation: Six petals.

Colour: Vermillion orange.

Auric Layer– Emotional Body

Site: Lowest point of spinal column, sacral plexus in the pubic region

Sense Organ: Tounge

Associated Sense: Taste

Work Organ: Genitals

Corresponding Gland: Gonads

Main Issues– Emotional Balance / Sexuality

Developmental Age– 7– 14 years

Vehicle of the Bija: Crocodile

Associated Deity: Shakti, Durga

Associated Planet: Moon, Rahu (Pluto)

Associated Zodiac Sign: Cancer, Scorpio

Related Essential Oils; Sandalwood, Clary sage, Cedarwood, Ginger, Juniper berry, Cypress, Jasmine

Associated Crystals– Carnelian, Pearl, Garnet Orange or honey Calcite, Moonstone

"SWADHISTHAN or SEXUAL" charka is associated with our emotional body, in the auric layer. It is most active during the age of 8 to 14 years (puberty age), responsible for development of sexual organs. This is the period the sensuality enters in a child's relationships allowing him/her to reach out to family and friends as a new awareness of the physical body evolves. This chakra denotes the "desire" center of the being. Desires for physical sensations and material things, play at persons mind making him/her restless and confused. This is related to procreation, material achievements, power seeking attitude and behavior. Positioned at pubic region, this chakra regulates gonads and sex organs, is responsible for the quality and quantity of sexual energy as well as its exchange between self and others at the physical, emotional and spiritual planes.

It is depicted as a six petalled lotus of vermilion orange colour. On each petal there is a letter: bam बं , bham भं , mam मं , yam यं , ram रं , and lam लं , written in the colour of lightening. The element associated with this chakra, depicted as a white crescent moon within the pericarp of the lotus. Swadhisthan is regarded as the substratum or basis of individual human existence, whose counterpart in the brain is the unconscious mind, the storehouse of our sanskaras (mental impressions). The animal associated with the Chakra is crocodile, which

represents the unconscious mind and its sensuous nature. Seated on the crocodile is the bija mantra vam वं . Within the bindu of the mantra is depicted deities Vishnu and and Rakini as a form of Shakti. Vishnu represents the power of preservation and sitting in the seat of procreation, depicted with four arms and blue body. Rakini Shakti is represented as two headed, representing the split of energy in this chakra, where a person is trying to attain a balance between the world outside and the world within.

The element associated with this chakra is water, which makes this chakra, prone to emotional swings. According to tantra our unconscious mind records each and every perception, association and experience, a quarrel or bitterness has a stronger registration. All these registrations play a part in determining our day to day behaviour, attitudes and reactions and pose a hindrance in our spiritual progress and kundalini awakening process.

The sanskrit word Swadhisthan comprises of swa meaning "one's own" adhisthan meaning "dwelling place", represents the true nature of the person. Besides the term "swad" also means 'taste' which is the sense associated with this chakra as you taste life through this chakra. This is the desire center of our body 'desires are not needs' but still rule some of us. Till the time, we are ruled by our desires we will always be unhappy, because you fulfill one desire and you have another one, always leaving you unsatisfied and unfulfilled. Therefore desires are the distractions in the path of our spiritual progress.

The vayu associated with this chakra is "Vyan vayu" which helps maintain circulation in the physical body. Physiologically Swadhisthan chakra regulates our reproductive and urinary systems, it corresponds to the hypogastric or sacral plexus of nerves and controls the unconscious in human beings. Imbalance or blockages in the sexual chakra results in the malfunction in the circulatory and the excretory system of the body resulting into problems associated with body fluids for e.g. blood, lymph, saliva, urine, menstruation, digestive juices and all the organs related to their production. Besides the imbalance results in emotional disturbances, as this chakra is the seat of emotions. A weakened Swadhisthan chakra is also a major precedent of lowered immune system, affecting heart chakra and leading to common as well as rare infections, as in the case of HIV–AIDS and cancer.

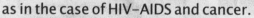

Carnelian

Garnet

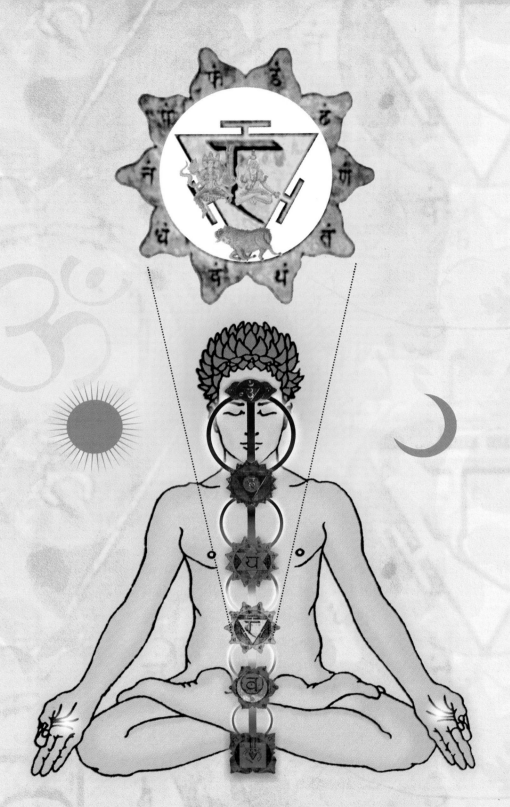

MANIPURA (SOLAR PLEXUS) CHAKRA

MANIPURA (SOLAR PLEXUS) Chakra

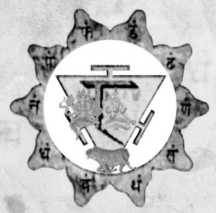

Guna: Rajasic

Principle Element: Fire.

Vayu: Samana.

Structural Representation : Ten Petals.

Colour : Yellow.

Auric Layer Mental Body

Site: below the diaphragm represents Solar Plexus

Corresponding gland: Pancreas.

Sense Organ: Eyes

Associated Sense: Sight

Work Organ: Feet & Legs

Corresponding Gland: Pancreas

Main Issues–Metal power/ Self Will

Developmental Age– 14–21 yrs.

Vehicle of the Bija: Ram

Associated Deity: Ram

Associated Planet: Sun

Associated Zodiac Sign: Aries, Leo

Related Essential Oils: Black Pepper, Rosemary, Chamomile, Juniper berry, Marjoram, Turmeric, Thyme

Associated Crystals– Ruby, Tiger Eye, Yellow Topaz, Citrine Yellow calcite, Pyrite and Sun Stone

"MANIPURA or SOLAR PLEXUS" charka is associated with mental body in our auric layer. It corresponds to the solar plexus, which is the seat of anxieties, and controls the entire process of digestion, assimilation and temperature regulation at the physical level. Most active during the age of 15–21 years, this chakra is responsible for the mental power and logical thinking. This is the phase when a person tries to seek his/her identity in the world, therefore governs the establishment of the Ego in the human realms with varying degrees of self assertion and its acceptability. The health of the Manipura Chakra determines the expression of the Individuality and it is here that the dissolution of karmic account begins in the spiritual path and thus the fire element.

The Sanskrit word Manipura originates from two words, 'mani meaning jewel' and 'pura means city' literally meaning city of jewels. In Tibetan tradition it is referred as jewelled lotus "mani padma". It is the seat of money, abundance, authority and power. Therefore, it is the seat of 'Ego' also. A person dominated by the third chakra will strive for personal power and recognition, even to the detriment of family and friends.

Manipura is symbolized as ten petalled lotus and on each petal is the depiction of ten letters pham फं, dam डं, dham ढं, nam णं, tam तं, tham थं, dam दं, dham धं, nam नं, pam पं. In the center of the lotus is the region of fire, symbolized by an inverted fiery red triangle which shines like a rising sun. In the lower apex of the triangle is the ram, vehicle of the bija, symbolizing dynamism and indomitable endurance. On this is placed the seed mantra ram रं. Those who are aware of Indian mythological epic Ramayan are aware that Shri Ram, around whom the whole epic revolves comes from the lineage of Sun hence called Suryavanshi. The element associated with this chakra is fire, symbolized as Sun. He was a king (the raja), this third chakra is rajasic; and the seed syllable is also his name–Ram, which is a very powerful mantra for Chanting. However the deities depicted in the center of the chakra are Braddha Rudra (Old Shiva) and Shakti Lakini. Old Rudra represents the power of dissolution, all that exists returns to him. In ancient yogic scriptures it is said that the moon at bindu secretes nectar which falls down to Manipura and is consumed by the sun, which results in the ongoing process of degeneration which leads to old age, disease and death. However, this process can be reversed in the human body by adopting certain yogic practices like kapalbhati, which can send the pranic forces from Manipura back up to the brain. The three heads of devi Lakini, symbolize her scope of vision encompassing three planes– physical, astral and celestial.

The sense associated with this chakra is vision, therefore associated with the sense organ eyes. However the organs of action are feet and legs, underlying the interdependence of vision, with the willful actions of legs and feet. The chakra is associated with the element fire, which aids in complete metabolic process including digestion and absorption of food, in order to provide our body the vital energy for its survival. The Vayu (energy) associated with the Chakra is Saman vayu which is balancing energy; it digests and distributes the essence of food to the entire body system. According to Sawar yoga, this chakra is an important junction where prana and apana vayu meet, maintaining the balance of the vital forces.

This chakra is considered as physical plane of existence, chakra and the astral bridge movement is upwards Therefore some of the the last on mortal plane or once Kundalini crosses this at the heart center its only towards crown chakra. tantric and Buddhist traditions consider that the actual awakening process happens at Manipura not at Mooladhara. As long as the evolution is in the level of Mooladhar and Swadhisthan chakras, the aspirant is stuck in mundane, like lotus is in the mud. Here the mud is our own physical needs, desires, mental and emotional problems. As soon as he transcends to Manipura he can see the whole perspective of things and possibilities of human consciousness.

Being associated with Solar plexus of nerves, this chakra is also the seat of anxiety. Since Solar plexus easily gets affected due to the chemical changes happening as a result of anxieties. The need to gain undue and illogical supremacy creates imbalance and blockages in the functioning of the chakra leading to raised levels of cholesterol, diabetes, ulcers, hepatitis, rheumatoid arthritis, heart diseases, and bowel dysfunctions. Also if, this chakra is unduly suppressed, it becomes responsible for imbalanced digestion, bad sleep and raised irritability. However, only at this plane the person starts seeking atonement of ones errors and moves towards higher plane by following the path of dharma, by remaining true to once nature.

Tiger Eye

Citrine

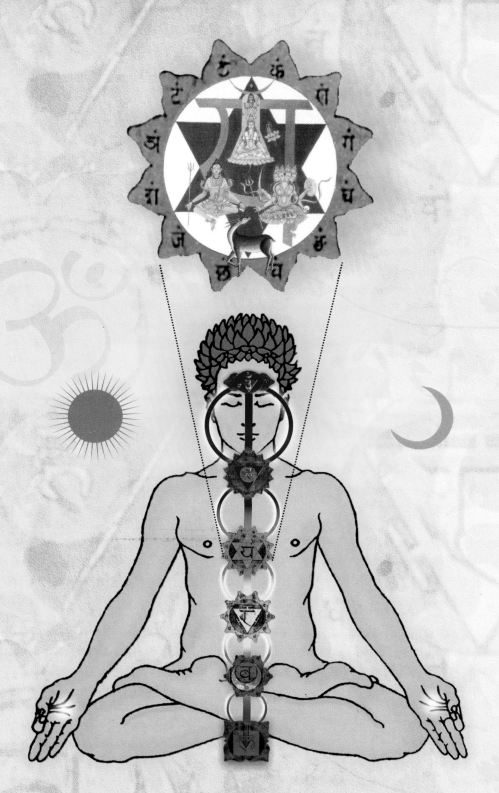

ANAHAT (HEART) CHAKRA

ANAHAT (HEART) CHAKRA

Guna: Sattvic.

Principle Element: Air

Vayu: Prana

Structural representation: Twelve petals.

Colour: Green.

Auric Layer– Astral Boady

Site: At the center and behind the sternum

Corresponding gland: Thymus

Sense Organ: Skin

Associated Sense: Touch

Work Organ: Hands

Main Issues– Love & Relationships

Developmental Age– 21-28 yrs.

Vehicle of the Bija: Deer (Antelope)

Associated Deities: Krishna, Hanuman

Associated Planet: Venus & Mercury

Associated Zodiac Sign: Libra, Taurus

Related Essential Oils: Holy Basil, Lavender, Eucalyptus, Tea Tree, Frankincense, Rosemary, Rose, Geranium

Associated Crystals– Malachite, Peridot, Zircon, Diamond, Rose Quartz, Emerald, Water melon Tourmouline. Green Aventurine, Chrysoberyl, Rhodocrosite, Amazonite and Kunzite.

The fourth layer or Astral body along with a very special "HEART or ANAHAT CHAKRA" is associated with our unconditional acceptance, love for us and all that forms the universe. It corresponds to the cardiac plexus of nerves and controls the functions of heart the diaphragm and other organs in the region, at physical level besides regulating the function of Thymus gland.

This is considered as the bridge at the astral plane between gross/ physical plane and the subtle/spiritual plane existing above the astral plane. Most active during the age of 21 to 28 years this is an important charka for the sustenance, and represents universal love, it plays an important role in our relationships. Its proper functioning enables us to accept without conditions, ourselves as well as those around us representing the need for the goodness of humanity.

It is represented as twelve petalled lotus and on each of the petals a letter is inscribed as : kam क, kham ख, gam ग, gham घ, ngam ङ, cham च, chhham छ, jam ज, jham झ, nyam ञ, tam ट and tham ठ. The inner region is hexagonal in shape, made up of two interlaced triangles symbolizing union of Shiva and Shakti. The inverted triangle is the symbol of creativity Shakti, while the upright triangle symbolizes consciousness or Shiva. Hexagonal shape represents element 'air'. The vehicle for the bija is black antelope, known for its compassion, alertness and quick movement, placed in the center of the hexagon above which is depicted seed syllable "yam" य. Within the center are depicted deities associated with the chakra as Ishana Rudra (Shiva the lord of northeast) and Shakti Kakini, benefactress of all, auspicious and exhilarated. It is said that below the main lotus of Anahat chakra is a subsidiary lotus with red petals, which contains a wish fulfilling tree called Kalp Taru. When this tree starts to fructify your wishes start to become true. Ancient sages had recommended visualization of this tree or a still lake with a blue lotus, within the Anahat hexagram.

Vishnu Granthi is the second of the psychic knots located at the heart chakra. It represents the bondage of emotional attachments, which according to Patanjali is again, a major source of imbalance as well as agony. Our biggest source of pain are the people and things we are attached to. And whenever, there is an attachment to results, the effort gets imbalanced and affects the desired result. This is what, has been preached by Lord Krishna to Arjuna in battlefield of Mahabharat, asking him to rise above his attachments. Lord Krishna (reincarnation of Lord Vishnu– the principle of sustenance) is considered to be the ruling deity. Anahat chakra can be energized and awakened by bhakti yoga as attachments and ego, are the only obstacles on the spiritual path.

The Vayu associated with the chakra is all vital Prana vayu, which is much more than the breath energy as this chakra also regulates all the organs of survival. The seed syllable for this chakra is " yam   ", which is also the name of the deity of death in Indian mythology. Another deity associated with the chakra is Hanuman (the monkey faced God), described as "Pawan putra" meaning 'son of air', the principle element associated with the chakra. He as a deity is prayed to remove all the fears, as Anahat chakra is also the seat of our fears. Development of Anahat chakra gives you the freedom to escape from a preordained fate and allows one to determine own destiny.

Anahat chakra is an important center for healers to develop compassion. By evolving through the fourth chakra, one masters language, poetry and all verbal endeavors for the expression of the feelings of the heart. Bhajans and bhakti yoga are the attributes of heart chakra. Imbalance in this chakra leads to mental attitudes like possessiveness, exaggerated self-importance or selfishness. Being related to the organ heart it affects all its functions, circulation of blood, volume of blood, lungs, tension, blood pressure problems, cramps, spasms, sometimes even Cancer and AIDS. Anahat Chakra is an important center for healers to develop compassion. By evolving through the fourth chakra, one masters language, poetry and all verbal endeavors for the expression of the feelings of the heart. Imbalance in this chakra leads to mental attitudes like possessiveness, exaggerated self-importance or selfishness. Being related to the organ heart it affects all its functions, circulation of blood, volume of blood, lungs, tension, blood pressure problems, cramps, spasms, sometimes even Cancer and AIDS.

Rose Quartz

Melachite

VISHUDHHI (THROAT) CHAKRA

VISHUDDHA Or THROAT CHAKRA

Guna: Sattvic

Principle Element: Ether

Vayu: Udana

Structural Representation: Sixteen petals.

Colour: Blue

Auric Layer- Etheric Template Body

Site: Hollow of the throat.

Corresponding gland: Thyroid

Sense Organ: Ears

Associated Sense: Hearing

Work Organ: Mouth

Main Issues- Communication & self Expression

Developmental Age: 28- 35 yrs.

Vehicle of the Bija: Elephant

Associated Deity: Five headed Shiva

Associated Planet: Mercury, Neptune

Associated Zodiac Sign: Gemini, Virgo

Related Essential Oils: Lemon, Bergamot,
Orange, Juniper, Sandalwood, Geranium, Cloves

Associated Crystals- Angelite, Aqua marine,
Turquoise, Amazonite, Blue Calcite and Celestite.

The fifth layer or ETHERIC template Body, along with the 5th chakra, the "VISHUDDHA" is associated with the Higher Will in association with the Divine Will. This chakra corresponds to the cervical plexus of nerves and controls the thyroid complex and also some systems of articulation, the upper palate and epiglottis. Most active during the age of 28 to 35 years, this charka governs communication powers of all types, verbal or body. It closely regulates heart function, as it regulates the thought expression processes. It stands for the captivating orator. Vishuddha chakra encompasses the five planes of jnana (awareness) thus bestowing bliss, it's here one receives communication of divine wisdom allowing him to seek knowledge which is true beyond the limitations of time, cultural conditioning and heredity.

Visshudha, is the sanskrit word originated from the word shuddhi meaning "to purify". Therefore this is the purification center. This chakra represents the higher faculty of discrimination, responsible for communication and self expression. This chakra is responsible for receiving or picking up thought vibrations from other people's mind. Any communication received even telepathically can be tested here for correctness and accuracy. In traditional symbology, it is represented as sixteen

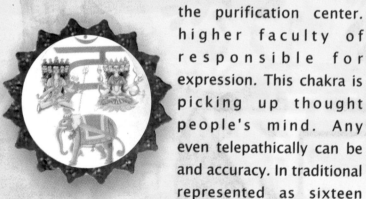

petalled lotus, the sixteen petals are also associated with the nadis represented at this chakra. Each petal has a Sanskrit word inscribed on it as am अं, aam आं, imइं, eemईं, umउं, oomऊं, rimऋं, reemऋं, lrimऌं, lreemऌं, emएं, aimऐं, om ओं, aum औं, am अं, ah अः . In the pericarp of this lotus is a circle representing element ether, within the moon shape of the chakra is the vehicle of the bija, snow white elephant with single trunk representing sound and pure consciousness. The seed syllable of the chakra is ham हं. The presiding deity depicted is five headed Shiva, five heads representing five elements in their purest forms. Also, five heads symbolize the five aspects of Shiva– Aghora, Ishana, Mahadeva, Sada shiva and Rudra. Shakti depicted here is Shakini, an embodiment of purity. This Chakra encompasses the five planes of jnana (knowledge) thus bestowing awareness and bliss, the Vayu prana circulates as vital force throughout the body.

Associated with the Vishhudha chakra is nadi called Kurma(meaning tortoise) nadi, once activated, the practitioner is able to overcome the desire and necessity for food and drink, as the practitioner can connect to the divine fluid secreted from Bindu, the point at the back of the head. Therefore Vishhudha is the legendry fountain of youth, once activated spontaneous physical rejuvenation can be experienced.

A well developed Vishhudha chakra endows exemplary communicating and oratory skills while an imbalance or blockage results in the most common loss of voice or hoarseness symptoms, the fear of being exposed. It affects all growth and development of the physical body, as it controls thyroid and parathyroid also problems of the throat like goiter, sore throat, asthma, temporary loss of voice and further suppression of expression of thoughts thus, leading to malfunctioning of the solar plexus.

Turquoise

Aquamarine

AJNA (THIRD EYE) CHAKRA

AJNA or THIRD EYE CHAKRA

Guna: Sattvic.

Principle Element: Panchmahabhut (All Five Elements)

Associated Sense– Sixth Sense

Structural Representation: Two petals.

Seed Syllable – Aum

Colour: Indigo/ White

Site: Between the brows, at the end of the nasal tract.

Corresponding gland: Pituitary

Sense Organ: Mind

Associated Sense: Sixth Sense

Work Organ: Mind

Auric Layer– Celestial Body

Main Issues– Wisdom, Intuition, Telepathy

Developmental Age– Not applicable

Vehicle of the Bija: Nada, also known as ardhamatra

Associated Deity: Shiva in form of Ardhnareshvar

Associated Planet: Jupiter

Associated Zodiac Sign: Sagittarius, Pisces

Related Essential Oils: Frankincense, Sandalwood, Camphor, Kewra, Rosemary, Holy Basil

Associated Crystals– Azurite, Lapiz Lazuli, Sodalite, & Flourite

Located between the eye brows, is the third eye of conscience. Two physical eyes see the past and the present, while the third reveals the insight to the future. All experiences and ideas serve only to clarify one's perceptions in Ajna chakra. The sixth layer or Celestial Body associated with an all important "AJNA" chakra is connected with celestial love, extending beyond the human range of love and encompassing all life forms. It stands for caring & support for the protection and nurturing of all manifested life forms, as representation of the divine one, the BRAHM. Ajna or Third Eye chakra also called Guru chakra (the guiding principle), as it connects us to universal intelligence. Tantra and yoga maintain that the Ajna chakra, is the command center and has complete control over ones life. It regulates the functions of pituitary (the master endocrine gland). Once the chakra is fully cleansed and opened for the first time it presents a state of non-duality – as one. In Ajna chakra the yogi himself becomes a divine manifestation, he embodies all elements in their purest form or essence.

The word Ajna Sanskrit root obey or to literally it command or monitoring According to scriptures  comes from meaning "to follow" means the center. spiritual this chakra is the seat of Guru, it is here you can hear the communication of inner guru. It is also called the eye of intuition or "divya Chakshu" (the divine eye) or the gyan netra (the eye of knowledge). Ajna is symbolized as a two petalled lotus, on the left petal is the letter ham हं, and on the right ksham क्षं, as the bija mantras of Shiva and Shakti. Within the lotus is the perfect circle symbolizing Shunya (Zero– as void). Within this circle, is an inverted triangle representing Shakti creativity and manifestation. Above the triangle is the Shiva lingam as symbol of our astral body (an attribute of our personality). Ardhnarishvara (half male and half female aspect of Shiva and Shakti) stand in the lingam, symbolizing the culmination of basic polarity. Next to the lingam is depicted Shakti Hakini with four arms and six heads. She imparts the knowledge of eternal truth and awareness of non duality. Over the shivalingam is the Bija Mantra Om ॐ the traditional symbol with its tail on top and the crescent moon and bindu above that.

This chakra is associated with the various cognitive faculties of the mind, both for the mental images and abstract idealism. The chakra is also the point of merging of three nadis Ida, Pingala and Shushumna. In mythology, these nadis are represented by three holy rivers in India Ganga as Ida, Jamuna as Pingala and Saraswati as Shushumna. When the mind is concentrated at this conjunction, transformation of individual consciousness happens and duality ends with the dissolution of ego. As long as there is duality there cannot be Samadhi, meaning as long as there is even a particle of ego further spiritual progress is not possible.

This is an essential chakra for developing higher intuition, clairvoyance, abstract thinking and higher mental faculty functions. Sluggish, dull body activities are a result of dull third eye chakra. Imbalance results into indecisiveness an attitude as well as a trait, also for not being responsible to ones actions. General allergy to everything– asthma and all diseases related to any endocrine gland.

Lapis Lazuli

Azurite

SAHASRARA (CROWN) CHAKRA

Journey through Chakras

BINDU & SAHASRARA (CROWN) CHAKRA
(Thousand Petaled Lotus)

Guna: Trigunatit.

Principle Element: Beyond all elements

Associated Sense- Beyond Self

Structural Representation: Thousand petaled lotus.

Seed Syllable- Aum

Colour: Golden (for therapy violet)

Site: At the center of the Fontanelle above the head.

Correspondong gland: Pineal body

Associated Sense: Beyond The Senses

Auric Layer- Causal Boady

Main Issues- Spirituality,Selflessness

Developmental Age- Not Applicable.

Beyond all forms and names, point of illumination

Associated Planet: Saturn

Associated Zodiac Sign: Aquarius

Related Essential Oils: Brahmi, Henna, Jatamansi, Rosemary,

Frankincense, Holy Basil, sage and Lotus

Associated Crystals- Blue Sapphire, Amethyst, Clear Quartz and Flourite

There are two other higher centers in the brain which are commonly referred to in kundalini yoga, bindu and sahasrara. Bindu, means a point a point, at the top back of the head, where hindu brahmins keep a tuft of hair. It is called Bindu visarga, which litrally means "falling of drop" represented as crescent moon and a white drop which is the nectar dropping down to Vishuddha chakra. From this point on the oneness divides itself into many; it feeds the optic system and since it is the seat of nectar or amrit.

Sahasrara is supreme, the seat of highest awareness. chakras are within the realms of psyche, while Sahasrara acts through nothing and yet again, it acts through everything. It is the center of super consciousness where all polarities integrate, thus passing beyond the ever-changing "Samsara". Opening of this chakra, is a state of transcendence and hence may be called the attainment of "Buddha hood", probably "enlightenment" or the "Sivsdasha", leading to spiritual state that transcends mundane realities into affinity and eternity, the state of "Advait" (oneness– where no duality exists).

The seventh layer or the Ketheric Template is associated to this highest most hakra, revered for its psychical representation of oneness with the one, the enlightened or the higher consciousness. Located at the top of the cranium or cerebral plexus Sahasrara synchronizes all colors (hence white light) encompasses all senses and their functions and has all pervading power. When the Kundalini is raised up to Sahasrara chakra, the yogi becomes realized and the illusion of individual self is dissolved. Sahasrara is the culmination of the progressive ascension through the different chakras. Up to the sixth chakra the yogi may enter a trance in which activity or form still remains within this consciousness, here in Sahasrara chakra the prana moves upwards and reaches the highest point, the mind establishes itself in pure void or Shunya (zero) the space between two hemispheres. At this place of total Void, holding the inverted thousand petalled lotus showering the subtle body with cosmic radiation. At this point all activities of the mind, feelings, emotions, desires are dissolved and yogi attains the state of true bliss SAT–CHIT–ANANDA (truth being bliss). As long as he stays in this physical body, he retains non dual consciousness.

Amethyst

HEALTH & CHAKRAS–

There are three planes of existence, namely Physical, Astral & Spiritual. The first three Mooladhar, Swadhisthan and Swadhisthan are termed as physical plane of existence, where in a person is derived out of his ego, physical, physiological needs and desires only. While the heart chakra relates to astral plane, wherein the process of transformation and ascension begins. And the final three Vishudhha, Ajna and Sahasrara are termed as spiritual plane of existence also correspond to the higher mental centers. Hinduism attaches as much importance to the mind and the soul, as to the body. Our health is the sum total of our life style practices and the balance of the five elements, as you can **SPIRIT** enhance your health as well as longevity by drawing the optimum energy through five elements.

Ancient teachings tell us that all human actions originate in the mind and as per the laws of Karma, the energy is neutral and we shape it through our expression of thoughts, speech and action, empowered with strong undercurrents of our emotions. Sickness is always a physical expression of the spiritual discord, which can be dealt at the subtle plane through the charkas. Our ancient sages had been able to view diseases and life problems as chakra imbalances and used this awaren ess as integral part of healing. In today's times we still have some true yogis, psychics and healers who are able to see our aura, chakras and view chakra blockages. Practitioners of energy healings are attuning themselves to play a bigger role in the basic universal healing process.

TOTAL HEALTH

BODY

MIND

All stress related disorders are described as psychosomatic in origin. Our health is directly related to the health of our chakras. A single negative thought can disturb our body's energy level and imbalance the charkas. Stress, anxiety, depression and all other psycho somatic problems are major result of imbalance of our chakras, ultimately manifesting in the form of physical ailments in our body. Stress related conditions affect our whole being therefore affect almost all our charkas, though certain charkas are more involved and need to be worked upon to eliminate the cause of the condition.

You can look out for early stress signals such as nervousness, irritability, neck pain, shoulder and lower back pain and disrupted sleep. As our stress level increases, our pulse rate also increases and blood pressure goes up. We may suffer from loss of appetite or grow very hungry, sweat a lot or feel cold, we may also an increase in stomach acidity, problems with digestion, difficult bowel movement etc. On proper scrutiny of the cause and symptoms you can easily assess which are the charkas involved and imbalanced.

There are two basic types of personality– extrovert and introvert; psychologists define them as A and B type. A type are more ambitious, enterprising restless and hardworking. B type is easy going, less outwardly ambitious and prone to procrastination. One of our spiritual Gurus, describes extrovert people as the one, staying in their Solar or Pingla Nadi most of the time, while people who are introvert, deeply engrossed in emotional thoughts and always complaining are staying in their Lunar or IDA nadi most of the time.* The former may get stress related conditions such as hypertension, peptic ulcers, cardiovascular disorders, even diabetes. The B type is more prone to psychological conditions as depression, listlessness, anxieties, insomnia and even death wish. Other stress related disorders are headaches, migraines, asthma, arthritis, sinusitis, anorexia, even sexual disorders etc. Life is interdependent and consists of the involvement of others like our parent, relations etc. We face stressful situations in our everyday life and develop our own way of tackling it. And we have to learn how to maintain balance. Looking at the causes of stress, we need to look into the following three aspects–

Childhood and Upbringing–

Love is the basic foundation, for the upbringing of the person, in this material world. We often overlook the early upbringing which impacts our mental perception and reaction to stress. We often ignore the fact, that how important it is to have a secure background from the very early stage of life. In order to grow up emotionally healthy, and be able to adapt to different situations in life, we need the nourishment of love, specially from our parents and also from siblings. Initial two to three years, we are intimately related to parents more so with the mother and everything revolves around being really wanted and accepted. This impacts our Base root as well as Sacral chakra the most, besides having effect on Solar Plexus, Heart and Throat chakra too. The emotional fulfillment we gain from being loved and understood is an antidote to stress, it also helps us to have a balanced sense of ourselves leading to happy and loving relationships as we grow.

INTRINSIC Factors or attitude–

Your attitude and behavior towards self and others is a very important factor in judging your stress level and chakra health. Stress results from selfishness and self importance, the two sides of primitive ego, which is the imbalance of our Manipura and Heart chakra. Though selfishness is the natural expression of our instinct for survival but exaggerated self-importance, self-centeredness and attachment to things and people are a definite source of stress.

EXTRINSIC Factors–

Our awareness of our bodies and minds is not as sharply developed, as it is about the instruments and gadgets, we use in our daily life. Our 'self body awareness' level is relatively low, we do not devote much thought to how we sit or stand, how we breathe, how is our heart rate, posture, how our minds work etc. The demands of external world preoccupy us and our actions are directly in response to these demands. In short we are more scattered than composed. Only when we experience disharmony in the working of mind and body that we recognize the need to attend to ourselves. It is only then, that we analyze our actions and reactions and search for an understanding of the working of our mind and body. Trauma or the triggering effect of a sudden event such as the death of a close relative or friend, failure in exam, loss of job, marital/ relationship break up, financial problem etc. make us look for answers in other directions like destiny, karma and so on.

TOOLS FOR CHAKRA HEALING

The holistic approach to health fully acknowledges the integration of mind and body. The wellbeing of one depends on the good health of other. Disease is an imbalance of the energies manifesting in the physical body, therefore healing through chakras, the energy centers at the subtle body helps considerably in the process of healing. chakras respond to all kind of healing techniques and therapies, which can help alter the state of mind as well as alter the vibrations at the subtle level. Today we have various holistic options available to us for managing our stress Viz. – Yoga, Pranyam (breath work), Meditation Aromatherapy, chakra Workout, walking and all light physical exercises. As the same approach is doesn't work with everyone, you have to choose the approach most suitable for your type.

Journey through Chakras

YOGA

Yogas citta-vritti-nirodh (PATANJALI [Samadhi pada] SUTRA2)

So well defined in four words the basic nature of yoga–
Yoga is the inhibition of the modifications of the mind.

For thousands of years the Yoga has been practiced as an effective tool to improve physical, mental and spiritual health. The word YOGA derived from the Sanskrit word Yuj, means union, the term is used to connote a variety of meanings. It covers the elementary training of body and its limitations to promote normal healthy and peaceful human activities. The aim of yogic discipline is not so much to cultivate the body for physical strength, quick reflexes or develop muscles but to create a mental make up, through poise, balance and mental endurance.

Scientists today ascertain that the intrinsic organic health of a human being is of prime importance along with the outer development of the body. This was realized thousands of years ago by the ancient Indian yogis. The practice of yoga has a substantial foundation in science. Yogic asanas accelerate blood circulation in the body and Pranayama abates carbon dioxide content ensuring sound health.

There are various types of Yoga involving Dhyana Yoga, Bhakti Yoga, Karma Yoga, Laya Yoga, Tantra Yoga, Hatha Yoga etc. Out of these Hatha yoga is a popular kind of yoga involving an eight fold path viz. Yama, Niyam, Asana, Pranayam, Pratyhara, Dharana, Dhyana and Samadhi practiced for the upliftment of body, mind & spirit.

YAMA means the rules to be followed by the practitioner in a society.

NIYAMA means the set programme to be adopted by the practitioner for personal development.

ASANA means a steady and relaxing posture.

PRANAYAM involves regulating the period between inhalation and exhalation, as also disciplining the complete respiratory process.

PRATYAHARA means withdrawal of senses, the five senses in a human being are sight (eyes), touch (skin), Taste (tongue), hearing (ears), and smell (nose) are the doors of mind connecting it to the outer world. In pratyahara these senses are closed and mind is turned inward.

DHARNA means fixation of mind on an object. Since mind is restless and keeps shifting its object of attention, here it is fixed on a single object.

DHYANA means meditation, training the mind into a state of thoughtlessness.

Out of these Yama, Niyam, Asanas and Pranayam are clubbed together as Bhairanga (or external) yoga generally practiced for mental and physical health. Dharna, Dhyana and Samadhi form the Antaranga (internal) yoga also called Raja Yoga, while the Prtyahara (withdrawl of the senses) is considered as a bridge between the two. Certain Hatha Yoga exercises, pranayam and Raja Yoga are used as tools of Kundalini awakening and grouped together by various teachers as a part of Kundalini yoga.

Yoga provides all-round benefits to a human being:

To maintain the purity of blood and elimination of toxins, both outer and inner cleanliness is indispensable. Scientists prescribe sun-bath, steam-bath, shower-bath, air-bath and to this the yogis include the nasal cleansing (neti), stomach wash (dhouti), the depuration of the alimentary canal (basti), the purgation of the intestines, the bladder, and the sexual organs (vajroli) Yoga exercises have a strengthening effect on the nervous system through its non-tiring physiological activities that bring about poise of body and mind. Unlike the normal workouts that concentrate more on the inflation of the muscles, Yoga takes care of every little part of the anatomy, and work on us at physical, mental and spiritual levels

Physical – Through healing, strengthening, stretching and relaxing the skeletal, muscular, digestive, cardio–vascular, glandular and nervous systems.

Mental – Through the cultivation of a quite and a peaceful mind, alertness and concentration.

Spritual – By preparing for meditation.
Yoga and meditation treat a person not merely as a mass of flesh and blood, but as a being with a soul. Doctors have come to recognize that this kind of treatment can give patients greater solace and better recovery. As soon as a person takes to Yoga and meditation, her life pattern, personality and diet changes. He attains balance of mind, body and the spirit, more in control of him self. He tends to become a puritan (sattvic) and tries to keep away from smoking, drinking and consuming non–vegeterian food. Yoga is "a combination of psychoanalysis, psychiatry and physiotherapy", and that it directly affects the hypothalamus – area of the brain controlling endocrine activity – in preventing cardiac attacks. This helps generate positive spontaneous energy, which helps the person correct himself, and think clearly.

1 – Tadasana   2 – Vrksasana   3 – Trikonasana   4 – Parsvakonasana

6 – Virabhadrasana II   7 – Parsvottanasana   7 – Parsvottanasana   9 – Uttanasana
                            (simple)   (full pose)

MUDRAS

"Mudra", are simply body and finger posture, like yoga it is an ancient discipline to rejuvenate the body, mind and  spirit. According to Ayurveda and tantra, most physical ailments are due to imbalances of five body elements. Mudras are the use of hand in scientific manner to achieve the equilibrium of basic these five elements– earth, water, fire air and ether. Some mudras are extremely useful for meditation and promote state of deep concentration and stillness of mind. Various mudras like Gyan Mudra, Jal mudra (Water), Ayanvayu mudra, Pran Mudra (Life Energy), Prithvi Mudra (earth), Varun Mudra, Vayu Mudra (air), Apan mudra , Shunya Mudra (Space) and Sun mudra are used for balancing body elements to heal the corresponding charkas.

GYAN MUDRA– It is one of the most important and widely accepted in yoga and

meditational practices. To attain this join the tip of forefinger and the tip of the thumb. To get the maximum benefits, hold together gently for 15 to 30 minutes.

Benefits: It purifies the mind of the practitioner, improves intelligence and wisdom. It helps lifts mood, relieve insomnia and depression giving a feeling of joy. Helps people with addiction to intoxicants and drug.

APAN MUDRA– Joining the tips of middle and ring finger with the tip of thumb forms the Apan Mudra. This Mudra is associated with our Mooladhar Chakra.

Benefits: Cleanses and purifies the body, facilitate discharge of waste material (urination and menstruation) from the body, releases negative energy. This is a very useful mudra for people who feel lethargic.

PRITHIVI MUDRA– Helps to increase earth element, hence activates root chakra it is also useful for people who want to gain weight. To attain the mudra, touch your ring finger at the tip of the thumb and press it little. Rest three fingers should be held straight and then keep your palms at your knees. Practice for 15–20 minutes.

Benefits: This mudra cures weakness of body & mind, increases life force and gives vigour to an ailing person. It also boosts self confidence and gives peace of mind.

VARUN MUDRA– To attain this mudra, join tips of little fingers and thumbs and keep rest three fingers straight. Keep the hands at the folded knees. Keep the palm tight while rest of the hand should be relaxed. Practice for 10–15 minutes everyday.

Benefits: It helps improve circulation, prevents dehydration, urinary problems and improves skin quality. It is a suitable mudra for Sacral or Sawdhisthan chakra and associated imbalances.

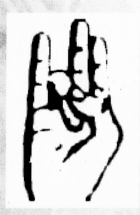

SURYA MUDRA– Join tips of both ring fingers at the root of both the thumbs. Allow the other three fingers of each hand to remain straight. Keep your hands at the folded knees, keep palms facing up. Put a little pressure in your palm and the rest of the hand should be relaxed. This mudra is useful for Manipura or Solar plexus chakra. It should be practiced for 10 to 15 minutes everyday.

Benefits: This mudra generates body heat and helps in digestion and weight control. It also relieves health problems like diabetes, regulates cholesterol and liver imbalances.

PRANA MUDRA– It is formed by joining the tips of ring finger and little finger with the tip of the thumb. This mudra balances all give Vayu (Energetic) in the body. It is recommended for Heart/ Anahat and all charkas above.

Benefits: Practice of Prana Mudra, energizes heart, improves the functioning of lungs, improves eye sight and revitalizes the body.

ABHAYA MUDRA: This is normally practiced after reciting Gayatri Mantra. Like in Gyan mudra, touch the forefinger to the tip of the thumb and raise your hands vertically to the side of your head. This mudra is useful for anxiety prone and fearful people, and helps balance both Solar plexus and Heart chakra.

Benefits: Mind becomes fearless, gives a feeling of courage and strength.

SHUNYA MUDRA: This mudra is attained by putting middle

finger of both the hands at the root of the thumb and press a little. Keep your hands on or near the knees with palms facing up, keep the position, for five to ten minutes. This mudra regulates space element hence useful for Throat and the charkas above.

Benefits: It strengthens heart, gum muscles, relieves tooth ache, earache. It also regulates thyroid gland functions helps in deafness and vertigo (giddiness).

MEDITATION

Mediatation is the integral part of Antarnga (internal) yoga; it is an effective tool to achieve the balance of mind, body and the spirit. Meditation does not mean, contemplation alone, it originates from Latin word– mederi meaning to heal. It meant to heal a mental affliction caused by psychological stress. Various teachers propagate meditation in various form but the ultimate objective is the same achieving the tranquil state of mind, devoid of thoughts and connection to universal consciousness. It may not be easy to achieve the state of thoughtlessness, as mind is drifting all the time. Certain practices, like charka meditation helps to steady the state of mind by initially focusing attention on each charka point and ultimately placing consciousness at the crown chakra.

Benefits of meditation include a greater sense of relaxation in both mind & body, greater flexibility of thinking, an ability to meet situation with freshness and insight. From the standpoint of pure physical expressio n it can help loosen the knots and tensions trapped in the body by distributing emotions. It can help to change both facial expression and body posture, thereby softening and strengthening at the same time. There are some of possible   results, but they are not the goals. Meditation helps strengthen the positive qualities of compassion, patience and wisdom and free us of conflicting emotions and erroneous beliefs.

There are many form of meditation: Silent sitting, chanting, praying, Walking meditation, meditation that uses visualization or focus on objects. Meditation can be found in almost every tradition in world if one were to look into their more contemplative practices.

Samadi is the state of highest equilibrium during meditation. When the individual consciousness merges into the cosmic consciousness. All limitations vanish, the individual consciousness empties itself and in that emptying process. Life changes, and daily living becomes a new and fresh experience.

Journey through Chakras

CHANTING (Japa) FOR CHAKRAS

Our subconscious mind carries millions of impressions, arising out of our Prakruti (Nature). The mind, intellect, subconscious mind (chitta) etc. are the constituents of Prakruti, and all these function according to their own characteristics and create their impressions. When we do any repetitive activity it sedates the mind and prevents its viriti (modification). Japa or chanting means repetition of some letter, word, mantra or sentence. Japa also has a derivative in _____

Meaning japa is that which destroys sins and liberates one from the cycles of birth and deaths. 'Namjapa' means repetition of a name that is chanting a deity's name. Mantrajapa refers to the repetition of a particular mantra. This path of spiritual practice is called– Namasankirtanyoga (Path of chanting Lord's name).

Ancient sages used to give Gurumantra to their followers, appropriate for each one, in order to balance their charkas, as they had the ability to see the aura and unders tand chakra imbalances. This is still practiced by some of the sages.

Today we have so much information available on mantras and chanting, market is also flooded with the audio tapes and Cd's of the mantra chanting, however it is very important to understand the energy and effect of the mantra before you can chant them. Bija mantras, associated with each of the chakra are easy to understand and follow hence excellent for chanting.

Then there are very potent mantras like Gayatri mantra– "Om bhur bhuwa swah, tat savitur varenyam, Bhargo devasya dhimahi, dhiyo yona prachodayat."

This mantra invokes the energy of Sun (fire element), it should be chanted with care, preferably early morning or late evening, in combination with other mantras to invoke earth (Prithvi Tattva) energy or water (Jal Tattva).

Chanting can be done by people of all religion and hues as per their faith and religious guidelines. Chanting the name of our Istha (favourite) deity, angel etc. also helps to balance the energies.

Chanting the names or mantras of the deities prescribed for each chakra is a common practice in Hindu culture, all deities are energies and by chanting and praying to the deities you invoke the energy of the said deity.

1.   For Mooladhar Chakra the mantra for the ruling deity Shri Ganesh is chanted–

"Om Shri Ganeshaya Namah"

or

" Om Shri Gan Ganpathaye Namh"

2.   Swadhisthan Chakra is considered as the center for procreation and Kundalini.

The Sanskrit word "kula" means family, kul devi is the form of energy (Shakti) who is the benefactor of the family or kul devata also represents the benefactor energy of the family deity. The particular form of these energies is determined by your ancestry, you are born into a particular family as a result of your past life karmas. Therefore the chanting mantra for the second chakra is–

Shri Kul deviyah namh   or Shri Kul Devtayeh namh

Alternatively you can chant the name of "Durga" the Sahkti–

"Om Shri Durga Deviyahe Namh"

3.   For Manipura or Solar Plexus Chakra, name of the deity Shrii Ram is chanted as under

"Om Shri Ram, Jai Ram Jai Jai Ram"

Alternatively, Gayatri Mantra as mentioned above can be chanted.

4.   Lord Krishna is an avtar of Lord Vishnu the principle of sustenance whose name is chanted for the balance of heart chakra–

" Om Namho Bahgwate Vasudevayah"

5.   For throat chakra the following hanuman mantra is useful–

"Hunm Hanumate Namh"

6.   Our Third eye Chakra is the seat of Guru, you can chant the name of Guru and invoke his energies as "Shri Guruvey Namh" alternatively you can chant the name of "Shri Gurudev Dutt" swarup of all the three deities (holy trinity) Brahma, Vishnu, Mahesh.

7.   For the crown chakra the chanting of any of the following mantras are useful. "Om Namo Shivay"   or   "Shivom" or "Om Soham"

People use Japa mala or rosary with 108 beads or half of it for chanting purpose though it is not necassry to use japa mala for chanting. There are certain guidelines for the use of japamala–

1.   One should not cross the "merumani"– the central bead, for that reason the rosary or japa mala is reversed after reaching the merumani. As the objective of this spiritual practice is to maintain the balance in Sushumna nadi. If you carry on in one direction you activate Ida or Pingla.

2.   The beads of the mala should be drawn towards oneself. The prana vayu is active when the beads are drawn towards oneself and saman vayu is active when you turn them away. Therefore you feel bliss when drwing rosary towards ownself.

Last but not the least– mere mechanical pronunciation of mantras is not deemed chanting. The pronunciation should be such that the seeker should get endowed with divine emotions and Lord's omnipotence. Patanjali describes only this kind of chanting, done with devotion, as "bhavana of the mantra". When a substance is repeatedly dipped in a solution, it gets fully deissolved into it. Similarly, when a seeker cahnts regularly, with devotion, he gets fully engrossed into it and merges with the mantra. This is the prime objective of chanting.

NADA, MUSIC (SOUND) THERAPY

The "Big Bang" is believed to be the precursor for the beginning of the Universe and life on it according to science. "OM" , the omkara in the Indian scripture is not a word but the very primodial "sound " at the beginning of all things to be manifested. This is also supported by the biblical reference of "The Word" which existed before anything else did. The word "universe" itself connotes to the "single rhythm in which the world is nurtured as a verse". Hence, Nada which means sound and music is the manifestation of sound in harmony.

Sound is the representation of energy vibrations and has the ability to alter the state of consciousness. Mystics and sages of old culture knew of the effect music could create for harmonizing, balancing and healing human energy. Music is a kind of 'Sadhana" (a spiritual practice) and had been practiced by "Gandharvas" (a group of Celestial musician). Bhakti yoga has two aspects– music created with devotion to Lord, and devotional songs. In India, Meera Bai known as the "singing saint " has been the symbol of devotion to lord Krishna through her melodious "bhajans" or the songs for the Lord. Similarly there have been many saints and seekers all across the world who have used music and devotional songs as the way to connect to Supreme Consciousness. Music and devotional songs do incorporate mantras, specifically bija mantras, but they are more than an extension of the repeated chanting of the mantras. Music is a vital energy which penetrates all forms of manifestations. We can use it to attain unity with the life forces and also use it to connect to the innermost core of all things. The raga (melody on Indian music scale) and the notes

of music can create different kind of effects on different people. It can have a calming and relaxing effect, as it brings about a balance of emotions and energy, it can also be stimulating and uplifting. The power of music can be assessed from the fact in ancient India Tansen was the musician in the court of Akbar the Great Moughal Empror; whenever he used to play raga deepika (igniting melody of lamp) at dusk all the lamps in the palace would get ignited automatically.

We can employ bija mantras with music, for individual chakras to attain the balance and healing effect of music. Different musicians and practitioners have used their abilities in this area and today all this work is easily accessible through audio channels and music strores. Like the bija mantras for each of the chakra, western music practioners use specific tones and keys for each of the chakra, for example-

The deep C and C major for the first chakra
D and D major for the second chakra
E and E major for the third chakra
F and F major for the fourth chakra
G and G major for the fifth chakra
A and A major for the sixth chakra
H and H major for the seventh chakra

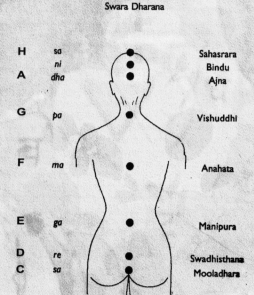

Western & Eastern Musical Notes corresponding to each chakra

Journey through Chakras

AROMATHERAPY

Each of us has an individual and unique sense of smell, which is one of the most powerful and instinctive of all our senses. Since ages we have relied on it for our choice of food, medicinal herbs, dangers of war, for religious / spiritual purposes, sex etc. Today we continue to use aromas to communicate our personalities and emotions, through the perfumes we use and gifts we give. When we take flowers to someone in hospital, we are using simple form of aromatherapy and colour energy to help them feel better. The bouquet contains essential oils that give its smell, helping to lift spirits. Aromatherapy is the modern name for using the plant essential oils to improve physical and mental well being.

In Indian mythological epic RAMAYANA, there is an anecdote wherein Laxmana, the younger brother of Shri Ram, had lost consciousness when hit by an arrow and he was revived by the Vaidya through the use of Sanjeevani booti (herb found abundantly in the Himalayas), which he was made to inhale. Lord Vishnu of the Trinity in Hinduism is also referred as Param Vaidya (the Supreme Healer). According to him medicine maybe used and administered in three forms, in ascending order of efficacy as in medicine in Solid form as Vatis (tablets) or Churan (Powder) , medicine in Liquid form viz. Syrups or Tisanes etc. and the most potent of all is the medicine in gaseous form which are mainly the essential oils of the plants, also referred to as the pranas of the plant. Essential oils have one of the highest energy vibrations and easily assimilated at the cellular level too.

ESSENTIAL OILS:

Essential oils are the most gentle of gifts from Nature to us. They are the volatile extracts of different parts of the plants like flowers, leaves, seeds, bark, wood, roots and even gum resins. They are the most potent representation of the plant's therapeutic and healing properties. They are highly aromatic and have balancing effect on our mind, body and emotions through inhalations and application on the body. Therefore used in various complimentary therapies since ages.

What human beings are to the animal world, the herbs are to the plant kingdom. As the five elements and three gunas are present in us, plants also have representation of three gunas (as in the roots, the trunk and the branches and the leaves and the flowering tops) and five elements. For that reason Ayurveda classifies certain plants and oils more Sattvic than others.

Five basic elements in Plants and use of their essences for chakra healing–

Earth– As earth element is associated with our root chakra, in plants it is associated with the roots. Similarly the oils from various plant roots are used to energize and balance the base root or Mooladhar chakra. Jatamansi (Indian spikenard) is a renowned essential oil used for Mooladhar as well as Crown chakra imbalances. Other useful oils are Angelica root, Valerian root, Costus root, Nagarmotha, Patchauli, Vertiver etc.

Water– Water element though associated with Swadhisthan or Sacral chakra is associated with the plant trunk, since trunk work as the water ways for the entire plant. Most useful among the oils for Sacral chakra are Sandalwood, Cedarwood, Ginger (a modified stem) etc.

Fire– The fire element is represented in our Solar Plexus or Manipura chakra is associated with the brightly coloured flowers and spices like black pepper and clove. Amongst other useful oils are Rosemary, Marjoram, Chamomiles, Lavender, Thyme, Fennel, Cardamom, Rose, Geranium, Lotus, Clary Sage etc.

Air– The air element present in our heart chakra is represented in plants through its leaves. The most revered plant for heart chakra is Holy Basil, other useful plant oils are Eucalyptus, Lotus, Rose, Tea Tree, Lemongrass, Rosemary, Frankincense, Lavender, Thyme etc.

Ether– Described as space or akash tattva (element) is associated with our Vishudhha or Throat chakra. In plant this element is associated with the fruits and the seeds. The useful oils are Lemon, Orange, Bergamot, Bayberry, Sandalwood, Lotus, Tea tree etc.

As our Third Eye chakra represents Panch mahabhoot (five basic elements), the plant seeds represent all the five elements. As the seed has all potentials of the plant, the seed oils, as per the property, can be used on all the chakras.

The essential oils, should be diluted in a suitable base oil. Lotus seed or black Til (Sesame seed) oil is considered as Sattvic base oils to be used for chakra anointments. The selection and dosage should be as per the assessment of a qualified aromatherapist having an understanding of chakra imbalances also. In case of doubts it is advised to use pre blended anointments, from a known source.

CHAKRA ANOINTMENTS & CHAKRA DHYAN
(Chakra Meditation)

Though the chakras are anatomically undetectable, they are linked to different systems of our body. Since each of our chakra controls certain organs and glands, the imbalance may result in physical, physiological or psychological disorders. Chakra anointments prepared with natural essential oils (like FM's "Aromatantra" chakra workout oils) accelerate the process of harmonizing and balancing the charkas besides helping to heal diseases, related to the organs / glands controlled by the chakras.

In case you have chakra anointments, you may meditate after applying these chakra oils on chakra points in the following order—

Please note that generally we use right hand for application of chakra oils on the front of the body, clockwise(Right to left) motion to energize the chakras and anticlockwise to decongest the chakras. Initially you can start with 3, then increase to 5 can go up to 7 rotations, follow the same sequence every time you use the chakra oils, each time you apply the chakra anointments. It is not necessary to wash hands if you are following the series as mentioned below, however excess oil hand or fingers should be wiped with a tissue.

First a drop of AJNA chakra oil to be applied at the third eye point between the eyebrows, you can use middle or ring finger of your right hand to apply, rotate 3, 5 or7 times in clockwise direction.

Then MOOLADHAR (Base Root chakra) oil, to be applied by middle finger at tail bone point (Coccyx) each rotation should be followed by a gentle push, repeat 3, 5 or 7 times.

After Mooladhar we graduate up to SWADHISTHAN (Sexual) chakra, the location for oil application is just above the pubic area, you can apply few drops of Sexual (Swadhistan) Chakra oil just above pubic area again 3–5 or 7 times.

MANIPURA (Solar Plexus) chakra, also covers your naval (minor) chakra, so MANIPURA chakra oil can also be applied 1 drop at the naval and few drops at the Solar Plexus area, gentle rotation 3, 5 or 7 times at the solar plexus area will also release stored up anxieties.

ANAHAT (Heart) chakra is located at the center of the chest few drops of the appropriate anointment should be applied in clockwise direction however people suffering from High Blood pressure should apply in anticlockwise direction.

Few drops of VISSHDHI (Throat) chakra oil to be applied at the center of throat in clockwise motion using your finger tips.

Now we come to SHASRARA chakra, which is located at fontelle of the head, use your palm for application of few drops of your anointment, close your eyes, take your consciousness to the chakra point and use your palm with gentle pressure to anoint the chakra point.

Once you have completed the process of chakra anointments, you are ready for meditation,
Please follow the step by step guidance provided.

CHAKRA DHYAN (Chakra Meditation)

Objective of chakra Dhyan is to balance your chakras for optimum health

<u>Benefits</u>– Balance of Mind, Body & Spirit, reflecting in your Physical, Mental & Emotional Health

<u>Posture</u>–

- Make yourself comfortable in a meditative posture (asana) preferably Siddhasana or Siddha yoni asana.
- Place both hands on the knees–palms facing upwards, thumbs and forefingers together.
- Close your eyes and make the body steady throughout, keep the spinal column upright and straight while the back and shoulders are fully relaxed.
- The whole body should be relaxed and immobile, maintain absolute awareness of the physical body for few minutes.
- Become aware of the spinal column, observe your breath for few moments (to the count of 10)
- Now bring your awareness to Ajna chakra, this chakra is located inside the brain at a point directly behind the center of our eye brows.
- Try to feel a pulsation within this Ajna chakra region. Be absolutely aware of this pulsation.
- Start chanting AUM (ॐ) with each inhalation, synchronize the chanting of Aum with the pulsation at Ajna chakra. Maintain this awareness of the pulsation at the Ajna chakra with the chanting of Aum, for some time, count this pulsation a few (5–7) times.
- Now shift your awareness to Mooladhar Chakra, exact location of this chakra is between genitals and anus.
- Now begin practicing Ashwini Mudra (contraction & relaxation of anus) a few (5–7) times at medium speed (contract hold till the count of 3–5 and relax)
- Start chanting the seed word for Mooladhar chakra " Laam" "ला..म " with each inhalation.
- Feel your breath vibrations reaching the Mooladhar chakra causing a return

pulsation at Ajna chakra. Which you'll begin to feel automatically after a few sessions.

- Now bring your awareness to the perineal region, the psychic center of Mooladhar chakra– try to feel the subtle pulsation at this point. Keep your focus there count a few times (5–7).
- Now you bring your awareness to your to Swadhisthan Chakra in the region of the tail bone at the back and pubic region at the front.
- Try to feel a pulsation in this region.
- Then begin the contraction and relaxation of genitals (Vajroli Mudra), Contract, hold to the count up to 3 to5 then relax.
- Now chant "Vaam" " ग..म " (seed word for Swadhisthan chakra) with each inhalation.
- Feel the vibrations of your breath reaching the chakra point, focus your attention there, count up to seven.
- Now feel the simultaneous pulsation at your Ajna chakra point. This will be automatic after a few sessions.
- Now shift your awareness to the naval region.
- Become aware of the psychic breath from Mooladhar point to the naval region and from the pit of the throat to the naval region.
- Both breaths should reach the naval point with complete inhalation, retain the breath there and develop mental awareness of this point, then exhale, repeat a few times.
- Now take your awareness to your Solar plexus point (in the hollow of your ribcage approximately four inches above the naval, feel the pulsation there.
- Start chanting "RA….AM" " ग..म " (seed word for Manipura Chakra) with each inhalation, hold the breath there to the point of 5 and exhale gently.
- Continue for few minutes or to the count of seven.
- Now bring your awareness to the center of your chest at the Heart Chakra Point.
- Feel the space in your chest and lungs filling up– contracting & expanding with the rhythm of your natural spontaneous breath.
- Try to feel the pulsation at your heart center you can even feel your heart beats.
- Chant "Yam" " या..म " (seed word for heart Chakra) with each inhalation and

feel the breath vibrations reaching to your heart chakra. After few sittings, you can even feel the simultaneous pulsation at the Ajna chakra point. Repeat few times (5–7).

- Now bring your awareness to the throat pit and then take it directly back to the neck at Vishudhhi chakra point.
- Feel each breath passing through your throat.
- The seed syllable for Vishudha chakra is 'Hum', ह..म which can be hummed in continuity as humming of a bee (as in Brahmri Rechak). You can feel the pulsations in the throat chakra and the resonance of your humming inside your head.
- Now move your attention back to Ajna Chakra, feel your breath vibration reaching up to Ajna chakra point, now make your breath deeper so as to send vibrations to your crown chakra at the center of your head.
- Now Chant " AUU....M" ओ..म moving your awareness from Mooladhar chakra and tip of the spine to Sahasrara at the top of your head.

Repeat seven times and then, let your awareness stay at your crown or Sahasrara chakra. This is the point of your connection with Supreme Consciousness.

Now visualize the golden light showering on you and FEEL THE TRAQUILITY FLOWING THROUGH YOU and stay with it in your state of meditation, as long as you desire.

- Rub your hands together gently, then over your eyes, face and head. Feel the Bliss.

CRYSTAL HEALING

Crystals have been used since ages for healing and balancing the body, mind and spirits, they can help to re-establish a broken link between mind body and the spirit. Today crystal healing is considered as a complementary therapy wherein the healer uses the crystal energy to enhance the healing process of the being. Each crystalline form has its own individual energy and its own personality. CRYSTALS, as mineralogical structures, contain more than one mineral, possess a melding of the energies of the mineral contained. Each can be used in unique ways to assist one in understanding the multifaceted nature of existence on this earth. The crystals have been used to act as catalysts, for healing and to assist one in becoming re-united with the source.

chakras are the source of physical, emotional, mental and spiritual energy and using crystals for chakra healing can have a great healing effect. Therapists using various forms of healing can combine crystals to enhance and accelerate the healing process. For example, a Reiki or Pranic Healer uses crystals during the healing process. Quartz and its varieties like Amethyst, Rose quartz, Smoky quartz etc. are most commonly used crystals for healing purpose.

CRYSTALS FOR MOOLADHAR or BASE ROOT CHAKRA

MOOLADHAR or BASE ROOT CHAKRA is associated with our etheric body and also with automatic and autonomic functions, since the chakra is associated with the physical functioning and physical sensation or feeling of pain and pleasure. Mooladhar is the first chakra in the spiritual evolution of man, where one goes beyond animal consciousness and starts to be a real human being.

The chakra is associated with earth element and red colour.It stresses the importance of being

Jaspers

Hematite

gro now". Its planet unded in the "here and is Mars and most useful crystal stones for this chakra are Red Coral, Red Jasper, Haematite and Agates preferably black, brown or moss agates. Some healers also use Smoky Quartz for healing of this chakra. Clearing a blockage in this area requires the visualization of white light entering the body at this point, with the crystal either directed towards the area or placed upon it. This chakra should be balanced in conjunction with Crown chakra.

CRYSTALS FOR "SWADHISTHAN or SACRAL or SEXUAL" chakra

"SWADHISTHAN or SEXUAL" chakra is associated with our emotional body. This chakra denotes the "desire" center of the being. Desires for physical sensations and material things play at persons mind making him/her restless and confused. This is related to procreation, material achievements, power seeking attitude and behavior. It controls the unconscious in human beings. Imbalance or blockages in the sexual chakra results in the malfunction in the circulatory and the excretory system of the body resulting into problems associated with body fluids for e.g. blood, lymph, saliva, urine, menstruation, digestive juices and all the organs related to their production. Besides the imbalance results in emotional disturbances, as this chakra is the seat of emotions.

Carnelian

Garnet

The crystals suitable for this chakra are Carnelian, orange Jasper, orange or honey Calcite, Moonstone and Garnet. Orange calcite is also a good stone to use. Clearing this chakra involves, circling the area in a clockwise direction with the crystal pointed towards it slightly. Visualization of a white light coming from the stone to this point is important. You can also use one or more crystals and place over the chakra point.

CRYSTALS FOR "MANIPURA or SOLAR PLEXUS" chakra

"MANIPURA or SOLAR PLEXUS" chakra is associated with mental body. It corresponds to the solar plexus, which is the seat of anxieties, and controls the entire process of digestion, assimilation and temperature regulation at the physical level. A person dominated by the third chakra wil l strive for personal power and recognition, even to the detriment of family and friends. Located at the Naval region this chakra

Tiger Eye

Citrine

represents Fire element and colour yellow, its planet is Sun and its stones are Tiger Eye, Yellow Topaz, Citrine, yellow Calcite, Pyrite, Sun Stone and Amber. Some healers also use rutilated quartz. The healing method is similar used for the 2nd chakra.

CRYSTALS FOR HEART or ANAHAT CHAKRA–

The fourth layer or Astral body along with a very special "HEART or ANAHAT CHAKRA" is associated with our unconditional acceptance, love for ourselves and all that forms the universe. Located at the center of chest, associated with colour Green, it influences air element and influenced by planet Mercury.

This chakra is an important center for the sustenance of the being. It is also an important center for healers to develop compassion. The stones suitable for this chakra are Emerald, Watermelon Tourmaline, Malachite, Aventurine, Amazonite, Chrysoberyl, Rhodocrosite and Kunzite. Rose and Rose quartz are also associated with this chakra, are frequently used by healers for this chakra, especially in cases involving relationship and emotional issues. Always use the crystal a few inches away from the body and a g a i n visualize white light coming from the stone directly to the point concerned. You can also use the stones

Rose Quartz

f o rplacing on the chakra point.

CRYSTALS FOR VISHUDDHA or THROAT

Melachite

CHAKRA–

The fifth layer or ETHERIC template Body, along with the 5th chakra, the "VISHUDDHA" is associated with the Higher Will in association with the Divine Will. This chakra corresponds to the cervical plexus of nerves and controls the thyroid complex and also some systems of articulation, the upper palate and epiglottis. Associated with the element ether and colour blue. This chakra represents communication and power of self expression. The stones suitable for this area are Aquamarine, Angelite, Blue Topaz, Blue Lace agate, Moon stone, Amazonite, Blue Calcite, Celestite and Turquoise. Use the crystal few inches away from the chakra and direct the white light through the stone, you can also place the stone near the chakra point.

Aquamarine

Turquoise

CYSTALS FOR AJNA or THIRD EYE CHAKRA–

The sixth layer or Celestial Body associated with celestial love, extending beyond the human range of love and encompassing all life forms. Ajna chakra stands for caring & support for the protection and nurturing of all manifested life forms. Located between the brows this Chakra is associated with sixth sense, colour Indigo and planet Jupiter.

The stones useful for this chakra are Azurite, Blue / yellow Sapphire, Lapiz lazuli, Sodalite, purple Fluorite and Amethyst. To clear the blockage in this area hold the crystal few inches way from the area, pointing downwards and should be rotated gently in a clockwise direction for several minutes. If you are using crystal placement you can place the crystal at chakra point and energize through there.

Azurite

Lapis Lazuli

CRYSTALS FOR SAHASRARA or CROWN CHAKRA–

The seventh layer or the Ketheric Template is associated to this highest most chakra, revered for its psychical representation of oneness with the one, the enlightened or the higher consciousness, known as the "SAHASRARA or the thousand petalled lotus".

Amethyst

However for therapy we use colour Violet, it is associated with planet Saturn.

The stones suitable for this chakra are Amethyst, Clear Quartz, Diamond, Gold Flourite and Sugilite. Point the crystal downwards towards the top of the head, turning in clockwise circles and again visualizing white light.

CRYSTAL WANDS– A wand is a single piece of crystal designed for specific use or a combination of various crystals affixed together to create a long tool for specific healing. Use of crystal wands for use on is gaining popularity. To create chakra wand chosen crystal stones for each chakra are fixed, at he the body of the wand (body of the wand can be made up of Quartz, wood, or copper) in the sequence of the charkas. On both end of the wand a high quality single terminated clear quartz is affixed alternative at one end a single terminated (pointer) quartz and on the other hand can be a small crystal ball, which can be used for reflex or acupressure massage. This wand can be used for aura cleansing and chakra healing, as well.

REFLEXOLOGY

Reflexology is again a popular non invasive therapy. Its philosophy and practice are similar to other zonal therapies like acupressure and acupuncture. Reflex zones are the terminal points or endings of nerves, and are directly connected to a distant organ or part of the body. The human body has a tremendous energy to heal itself, this healing energy surges through the body in specific pathways and could be tapped at different points which are called Reflex points. This simple technique helps us maintain good health and vitality as health is the natural state of being.

Reflexology is not only a treatment but also a diagnostic indicator of diseases in some cases, in their early stages. The massage on the reflex points has a definite effect on the internal organs. When pressure is applied on the reflex points, the functioning of the corresponding internal organs could be rectified and regulated, as the reflexive action of the nervous system that transmits impulses of all stimuli

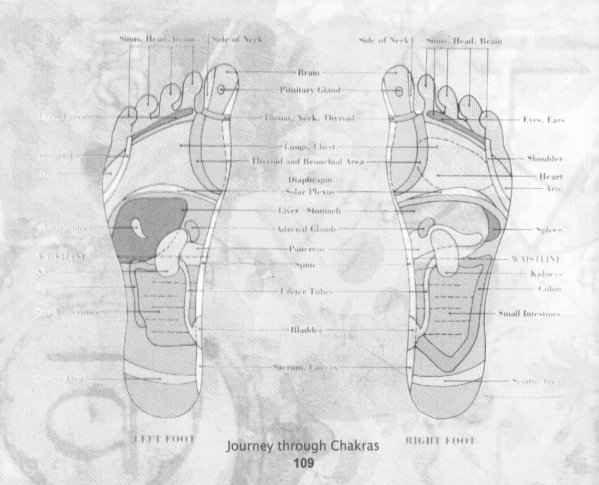

Journey through Chakras

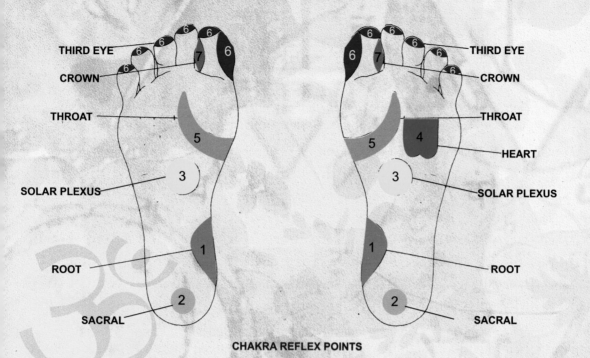

CHAKRA REFLEX POINTS

takes place within the entire body. In reflexology pressure massage may be given over the tender point for 1–2 minutes, the pressure could be maintained constantly or intermittently and beneficial result is achieved. Though reflexology treatment is not "a cure all", but it initiates a change in consciousness and removal of neural blockages thereby setting the ball rolling for self healing. Multiple sittings provide long term health benefits.

All matter is in vibrational state– whether visible or invisible. The vibrations of each single chakra can also be harmonized and intensified through the energy activation in the corresponding reflex zones. Even essential oils or chakra anointments can be used in chakra reflex massage. Therefore chakras are an integral part of reflexology, as you find representation of various organs and glands, you can identify the chakra points related to those organs in the same areas, reflex massage on the appropriate chakra zone helps healing and balancing of charkas. To initiate any healing sessions, the therapist begins by activating the core trilogy of charkas i.e. the heart center, the throat center and the solar plexus. This sets the body's own healing mechanism into active participation for furthering the benefits of the session.Herein knowledge, experience and intuition of the healer plays an important role in raising and balancing the energy. In this field the work of Marianne Uhl has been quite impressive.

ENERGY HEALINGS

Since time immemorial, energy healing had been practiced by ancient sages and priests, who were able to visualize chakras and the aura. In recent time various energy healing techniques are gaining popularity, especially Reiki and Pranic Healing.

Reiki is the Japanese term for the transcendental spirit. In Reiki the universal life force energy is used for healing and emotional blocks. There are various stages of energy amplifications, herein a practitioner acts as an open energy channel. This requires very high level of attunement and the practitioner is required to go through various levels of attunement

Pranic healing is an ancient science and art of healing utilizing prana, the vital energy also called – ki or chi to heal the body, mind and spirit. The basic tenet of pranic healing is that a human body is basically composed of two parts, the visible physical body and the energy body, also known as bio plasmic body. The physical body and bioplasmic body, are different aspects of human body. There are two basic principles of pranic healing, the cleansing, and the energizing of the patients bio plasmic body, with prana or vital energy.

In all energy healings, it is very important that the healer himself is healthy and have true intention of healing. In energy healings the healer is just a channel, like a water pipeline attached to the tap or source, if the pipeline is corroded or dirty, it will always affect the quality of water or energy at the other hand.

COLOUR THERAPY

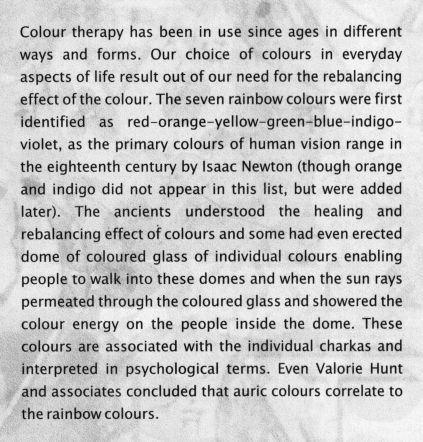

Colour therapy has been in use since ages in different ways and forms. Our choice of colours in everyday aspects of life result out of our need for the rebalancing effect of the colour. The seven rainbow colours were first identified as red-orange-yellow-green-blue-indigo-violet, as the primary colours of human vision range in the eighteenth century by Isaac Newton (though orange and indigo did not appear in this list, but were added later). The ancients understood the healing and rebalancing effect of colours and some had even erected dome of coloured glass of individual colours enabling people to walk into these domes and when the sun rays permeated through the coloured glass and showered the colour energy on the people inside the dome. These colours are associated with the individual charkas and interpreted in psychological terms. Even Valorie Hunt and associates concluded that auric colours correlate to the rainbow colours.

The seven rainbow colours are the most commonly used and associated with chakras and chakras healing. Mooladhar chakra had been associated with the most basic or primary colour RED. Different people have different interpretation of Red colour but mostly it is identified with life. Swadhisthan or Sacral chakra is associated with ORANGE colour, which is a composite colour having parts of earth's Red and Sun's yellow, symbolizing the beginning of polarity at this chakra.

Colour Yellow is associated with Manipūra or Solar Plexus chakra representing the ambivalence like sun also represents power, insight and intelligence. Green the colour of growth as well as healing is associated with our Heart or Anahat chakra. The colour blue is associated with Throat or Vishhudha chakra, it symbolizes truth and loyalty. Colour Indigo associated with Ajna or third eye chakra, as a mix of blue and violet symbolizes the end of polarity (ego) and unity (self). Violet associated with crown chakra, symbolizes unification, like the colour of root chakra mixed with blue, the colour of first highest chakra.

For chakra healing colour visualization with the corresponding chakra colour and simultaneous meditation on the chakra points is practiced. Consider these colours and meditatively draw the colour and tone, breathe each colour of your choice into appropriate chakra for atleast five breaths. However, some people may visualize different colours in the aura and charkas that is true for them and accepted. It is not unusual for many who cannot really visualize colours in particular, here the intent upon the colour works as well. The safest and the best way is to invoke the abundant White Light, available freely to all. The white light, is actually the most balanced mixture of all the seven colours and the shades in between. For self healing, invoking this beautiful healing light to work within, without one's mental restrains works better, as the White Light works with an intelligence of its own, far more purified than our limited awareness.

THE LAST WORD

Through this book we have tried to present the fundamental information on the chakras and various ways of healing and balancing chakras. Each of the healing and balancing technique mentioned in the book requires an in depth study and the heart of the healer. We hope this will be the beginning of the Journey for the seekers as well as the healers, there is still much more to learn and unlearn in the process of learning.

This reminds of an award winning advertisement of Brahmkumari's Meditation stating-
"Embark on a journey, where you are bound to lose all your baggage."

In this journey of life we are all carrying our baggages of material desires, attachments, greed, hatred, jealousy etc. In our spiritual quest we all have to lighten ourselves up to ascend at a higher spiritual plane. As mentioned earlier, chakras are best understood as levels of conscious awareness, not morality. Impurities also have to be understood from the level of discrimination not morality. Impurities arise out of desire, self-gratification and self-interest. There is much more to life than fame, fortune, status, authority and attachments to things or people. All pain comes to us through ignorance and staying blind when experience tells us something different. In the process of birth, the consciousness dawns on us from subtle to gross level, then we seek to raise ourselves from gross to subtle.

Hari-om Tat-sat

Glossary of Terms

Agni: fire.

Ajna charka: the psychic command center situated between the brows.

Akasha: ethereal space,

Amrit: psychic nectar which is secreted in drops from the lalana chakra to vishuddha charka, causing a feeling of blissful intoxication.

Apana: vital energy in the lower part of the body, below the navel.

Asana: a steady and comfortable position of the body.

Astral body: the subtle, psychic body, finer than the physical body.

Avatara: divine incarnation.

Awareness: the faculty of consciousness.

Bandha: psycho muscular energy lock which redirects the flow of psychic energy in the body.

Bhajan: devotional song.

Bhakta: one who follows the path of bhakti yoga.

Bhakti yoga: the yoga of devotion.

Bhrumadhya: the eyebrow center, kshetram or contact point for ajna chakra.

Bija mantra: seed sound; a basic mantra or vibration which has its origin in trance consciousness.

Bindu: the psychic center situated at the top back of the head; a point or drop which is the substratum of the whole cosmos, the sea of total creation.

Brahma: the divine spirit, hindu god; creator of the universe.

Brahma granthi: knot of creation. Psychomuscular knot in the perineum which must be released for kundalini to enter and ascend through sushumna nadi. It symbolizes the blockage posed by material and sensual attachment.

Brahma nadi: the most subtle pranic flow within the sushumna nadi.

Brahmin: a member of the highest hindu caste, namely the priestly caste.

Buddhi: the higher intelligence, concerned with real wisdom; the faculty of valuing things for the advancement of life and conscious awareness.

Causal body: the body you experience in deep sleep and in certain types of Samadhi.

Central canal: the hollow passage within the spinal cord. In the subtle body, this is the path of sushumna nadi.

Cerabral cortex: grey matter on the surface of the brain responsible for higher mental functions.

Cerebrospinal fluid (CSF) ;cushion of fluid protecting the brain and spinal cord.

Cervical plexus: automatic nerve plexus in the neck associated with vishuddha chakra.

Cervix: the circular opening leading into the womb; seat of the mooladhar chakra.

Chakra: literally 'wheel or vortex' major psychic center in the subtle body, responsible for specific physiological and psychic functions.

Chitta: mind; conscious, subconscious and unconscious levels of the brain.

Coccygeal plexus: a small nerve plexus at the base of th spine behind the pelvic cavity, related to swadhistan chakra.

Consciousness: the medium of the universal and individual awareness.

Deity: a form of divinity, a divine being having subordinate functions.

Devata: divine power.

Devi: a goddess; a manifestation of shakti.

Dharana: concentration; continuity of mental process on one object or idea without leaving it.

Dhyana: meditation, in the sense of intense meditation for an extended period of time.

Durga: Hindu goddess; a personification of Shakti, pictured riding upon a tiger, to whom personal ambition is rendered.

Ganga: the river Ganges, the longest and most sacred river in India.

Granthis: the three psychic knots on the susuhmna nadi which hinder the upward passage of kundalini- brahma granthi, Vishnu granthi and rudra granthi.

Gunas: the three qualities or matter of prakruti- tamas, rajas and sattva.

Guru: literally 'he who dispels darkness', the spiritual master or teacher.

Guru chakra: another name for ajna chakra, the eye of intuition; through which the inner guru's guidance manifests.

Gyana yoga: path of yoga concerned directly with knowledge, self-awareness.

Gyanendriyas: the organs of knowledge or sensory organs such as eyes, ears, nose, etc.

Hatha yoga: a system of yoga which specially deals with practices for bodily purification.

Hypothalamus: portion of the brain that integrates temperature, sleep, food intake, development of sexual characteristics and endocrine activity.

Ida: major psychic channel which conducts manas shakti, mental energy, located on the left side of the psychic body; the 'ha' of the hatha yoga.

Idriyas: sense organs.

Jalandhara lingum: symbol, vision of god.

Japa: chanting

Kali: form of Shakti who arouses terror and fear; destroyer of ignorance in her devotees.

Karma: actions, work, the inherent subconscious imprints which make a person act.

Karma yoga: action performed unselfishly, for the welfare of others and the fulfillment of dharma.

Karmendriyas: organs of action, e.g. feet, hands, vocal chords, anus, sexual organs, etc.

Khechari mudra: mudra of hatha yoga and tantra, in which the tongue passes back into pharynx to stimulate the flow of amrit from lalana chakra, activating the vishuddha chakra.

Kumbhaka: breath retention.

Kurma nadi: nadi associated with vishuddha chakra. It's control brings the ability to live without physical sustenance.

Limbic system: group of structures in the brain associated with certain aspects of emotion and memory.

Lingam: symbol representing Lord Shiva, the male aspect of creation; symbol of astral body.

Loka: world, dimension, or plane of existence or consciousness.

Lord shiva: Archetypal renunciate and yogi who dwells in meditation high in the Himalayas; Hindu God; destroyer of the universe.

Mala: a rosary-like string of beads used in meditational practices.

Manas: one aspect of mind; the mental faculty of comparing, classifying and reasoning.

Manas shakti: mental force.

Mantra: a sound or a series of sound having physical, psychic or spiritual
Potency when recited in a certain prescribed manner.

Marg: path.

Maya: principle of illusion.

Moksha: liberation from the cycle of births and deaths.

Moolabandha: yogic practice of stimulating mooladhara chakra for the awakening of kundalini. It is practiced by contracting the perineum in males, or the cervix in females.

Mudra: a psychic attitude often expressed by a physical gesture, movement or posture, which affects the flow of psychic energy in the body.

Nada: sound, especially inner sound.

Nada yoga: the yoga of subtle sound.

Neti: hatha yoga cleansing technique in which warm saline water is passed through the nasal passages; one of the shatkarmas.

Nirvana: enlightenment, Samadhi; harmony between the individual consciousness and the universal consciousness.

Om: the underlying sound of creation; the mantra from which all others have come.

Parasympathetic nervous system: division of the autonomic nervous system concerned with restorative processes and relaxation of the body and mind.

Pashu: the instinctual or animal aspect of human behavior.

Pineal gland: small pine-shaped endocrine gland in the midbrain directly behind the eyebrow center; the physical correlate of ajna chakra.

Pingala: the conductor and channel of pranshakti or vital force, located on theright side of the psychic body; the 'tha' of hatha yoga.

Prakruti: the basic principle or substance of the entire phenomenal or manifest world composed of the three gunas or attributes.

Prana: the life force in the body; bio energy in general; the vital energy which operates in the region of the heart and lungs; the psychic equivalent of the physical breath.

Prana shakti: pranic or vital force.

Pranayama: yogic practice of manipulating and controlling the flow of prana in the subtle body by controlling the respiratory process.

Purusha: consciousness; the spirit or pure self.

Rudra granthi: the knot of Shiva. This is the psychic knot within the ajna chakra, which symbolizes attachment to siddhis or higher mental attributes which must be transcended before full awakening of kundalini can occur.

Sacral plexus: nerve plexus in the back wall of the pelvis associated with swadhisthana and mooldhara charkas, and responsible for the functioning of the urinary and reproductive systems.

Sadhaka: a disciple.

Sadhana: spiritual discipline or practice.

Sadhu: a holy man.

Sahasrara: the thousand petalled lotus or chakra manifesting at the top of the head; the highest psychic center; the threshold between psychic and spiritual realms which contains all the charkas below it.

Samadhi: state of being above mortal existence; all-knowing and all-pervading state of being; the fulfillment of meditation; state union with the object of meditation and the universal consciousness.

Samana: vital energy operating in the region of the navel.

Sankalp: spiritual resolve.

Sankalpa shakti: will power.

Satsang: spiritual guidance, discussion and instruction from a guru.

Sattva: one of the three gunas of prakruti; the pure or equilibrated state of mind or nature.

Shakti: power, energy; the feminine aspect of creation.

Shambhavi mudra: mudra name after Shambhu or Shiva focusing the eyes on bhrumadhya.

Shanti: peace

Shivalingum: oval-shaped stone which is the symbol of Shiva consciousness or astral body.

Shuddhi: purification.

Siddha: adept, yogi; one who has control over nature, matter and mind.

Siddhi: perfection.

Solar plexus: intersection of a group of nerves in the abdominal region; the physical manifestation of Mmanipura chakra.

Soma: a plant used by the Rishis of ancient India for the purpose of spiritual awakening and mortality.

Sushumna nadi: the most important psychic passageway. It flows in the central canal within the spinal cord.

Swami: one who is the master of his own mind.

Swara yoga: the science of the breath cycle.

Swayambhu: self-created.

Sympathetic nervous system: the division of autonomic nervous system responsible for maintaining physical activity of the organ systems and expenditure of energy.

Tamas: darkness; inertia.

Tanmantra: the fives sense–sight, hearing, taste, touch, smell and the sixt sense.

Tantra: the ancient science which uses specific techniques to expand and liberate the consciousness from its limitations.

Tapasya: the practice of austerity; purifying the body off deficiencies and weaknesses.

Trataka: the meditational yoga technique which involves steadily gazing at an object.

Trishula: the three prolonged implement held by Lord Shiva; it symbolizes the three nadis.

Udana: the vital energy operating above the throat.

Uddiyana bandha: literally 'flying upwards'; a yogic practice of pranic manipulation utilizing the abdominal muscles and organs.

Vairagya: non–attachment

Vajra nadi: the nadi which connects the expression of sexual energy with the brain and is concerned with the flow of ojas, the highest form of energy in the human body which is concentrated in the semen.

Vajra mudra: contraction of the vajra nadi.

Vasana: the desires that are the driving force behind every thought and action of life.

Vayu: air.

Vedanta: the ultimate philosophy of the Vedas.

Vedas: the oldest religious texts of the Aryans written more than 5000 years ago.

Vishnu: Hindu god; preserver of the universe.

Vritti: a modification arising in consciousness, likened to the circular wave pattern emanating when a stone is dropped into a still pool of water.

Vyana: vital energy which pervades the whole body.

Yantra: a symbolic design used for concentrations and meditation; the visual form of a mantra.

Yoga: methods and practices leading to the union of individual human consciousness with the divine principle.

Yoga nidras: psychic sleep; yogic practice in which one can raise oneself from the mudane state of the body consciousness.

Yoga sutras: text written by Patanjali, delineating the eightfold path of the raja yoga, the systematic path of meditation which culminates in the Samadhi experience.

BIBLIOGRAPHY

Arnold Bitt Linger, "Archetypal Chakras", New Age Books, 2003.

Barbara Ann Brennan, "Hands of light", Bantam Books, U.S.A, 1988.

Dr. David Frawley, "Tantric Yoga and The Wisdom Goddess", Motilal Banarasidas Publishers Pvt. Ltd, 1996.

Dr. David Frawley and Dr. Rasant Lad, "The Yoga of Herbs", Motilal Banarasidas Publishers Pvt. Ltd, 1996.

Dr. J.K. Sarkar, "Anatomical and Physiological Basis of Rajayoga", Appendix-2: "Saundarya Lahri of Sri Sankaracharya", Sri Ramkrishna, Math.

Dr. Jayant Balaji Athavale and Dr. (Mrs) Kunda Jayant Athavale, "Science of Spirituality", vol.1-21, Sanatan Bharatiya Sanskruti Sanstha, 1998.

Dr. Ravi Ratan, "Handbook of Aromatherapy", Institute of Holistic Health Sciences, 2006.

Harish Johari, "Chakras, Energy centers of Transportation", Inner Traditions, India, 1987.

Harish Johari, " Dhanwantri", Rupa and co., India, 2003.

I.K. Taimini, "The Science of Yoga", the theosophical Publishing house, India, 1999.

Kenin Sullivan, "The Crystal Handbook", Penguin Books, 1987.

Marianne Uhl, "Chakra Energy Massage", New Age Books, 2000.

Melody, "Love is in The Earth- A kaleidoscope of Crystals", Earthlane Publishing house, 2005.

Pandit Gopi Krishna, "Kundalini, Path to Higher Consciousness", Orient Paper Backs, 2003.

Robert E. Svobode, "Aghora 2- Kundalini", Rupa and co., 1999.

Ruth White, "Chakras- A New approach to healing your life", India Book Distributors, 2003.

Swami Sivananda Radha, "Kundalini yoga", Motilal Banarasidas Publishers Pvt. Ltd., Delhi, India, 1992.

Swami Satyananda Saraswati, "Kunadalini Tantra", Bihar School of Yoga, India, 1996.

Dr. Ravi Ratan & Dr. Minoo Ratan
Offer

- **CHAKRA ASSESSMENT**

- **Chakra Healing/Balancing**

- **Energy Field Imaging**

- **HEALTH CONSULTANCY & Psychotherapy**

- **BODY THERAPY & TREATMENTS**

- **TRAINING PROGRAMS On AROMATHERAPY, CRYSTALS & CHAKRA HEALINGS**

At various healing  **Centers in**

UK, USA, Canada, UAE and in INDIA at-

F.M's MIND BODY CENTER
6th Flr. Doctor House, Peddar Road,
Opp. Jsalok Hospital, MUMBAI-400 026
Ph. +91-22- 24123678, 56648021/22, 65256032
Mob.- 9867318010 (Dr. Ravi Ratan)
9820428724 (Dr. Minoo Ratan)

email- fmsaroma@yahoo.co.uk/ * aromatantra@yahoo.com
website- www.fmaromatherapy.com * www. Aromatantra.com
Also available Aromatherapy Essential/ Base Oils, CHAKRA

Anointments. Skin, Hair & Health Care Products & Crystals.